DATE DUE

TO MAKE ALL LAWS

☆ ☆ ☆ ☆ ☆ ☆

THE CONGRESS OF THE UNITED STATES

1789-1989

☆ ☆ ☆ ☆ ☆ ☆ ☆

JAMES H. HUTSON

With a Foreword by
Thomas P. O'Neill, Jr.

Houghton Mifflin Company / Boston

This book was first published by the Library of Congress in 1989.
Except where otherwise indicated, all the illustrations in this book
have been drawn from the collections of the Library of Congress.

Library of Congress Cataloging-in-Publication Data

Hutson, James H.
To make all laws : the Congress of the United States, 1789–1989 /
James H. Hutson.
p.   cm.
Reprint, with new foreword and pref. Originally published :
Washington : Library of Congress, 1989.
ISBN 0-395-53560-3
1. United States. Congress.   I. Title.
JK1061.H86   1990   90-4661
328.73—dc20   CIP

Printed in the United States of America

WOZ 10 9 8 7 6 5 4 3 2 1

CONTENTS

THE INSTITUTION
AND ITS MEMBERS

MILESTONES

FOREWORD

Since Congress first convened two hundred years ago, it has been the subject of much public comment — usually unfavorable. In spite of this public scrutiny, historians seem to prefer to study the presidency rather than Congress. Modern journalism also spends much more of its time and resources covering what a president says rather than what a Congress does. The bicentennial anniversary of the first Congress brings some welcome attention to Congress and its achievements. *To Make All Laws* is a candid, knowledgeable, and insightful review of the Congress of the world's greatest democracy.

The genius of the Founding Fathers can be recognized in the fact that the Constitution that successfully served a militarily weak, sparsely settled, and isolated eighteenth-century agricultural nation continues successfully to serve the needs of a vast, populous, industrialized nation that is also a world superpower. American democracy may not be efficient, but it certainly is resilient. In the face of wars and depressions, scandals and controversy, the American people have chosen their political leaders through the discipline of the ballot box, accepting the results with remarkable good humor on most occasions.

As a member of Congress and eventually Speaker of the House, I was always surprised by how little most voters thought of Congress and yet how highly they regarded their own congressman or congresswoman and their own senators. Unlike individual members of Congress, the Congress *as an institution* is not easy for the public to know and to understand. The presidency speaks with one voice, and the Supreme Court (although with dissenting opinion) renders one decision; but the Congress is voting, debating, amending, and extending discussion all the time. It speaks with 535 voices that are seldom in unison.

The voices in Congress that are clear and understandable to voters are those of their local congressional leaders; as a result, individual representatives, not the institution as a whole, are heard and respected. The bond between voters and their representatives in Congress is strong because, as I am fond of reminding people, "all politics is local." Modern technology is also now making it possible for members of Congress to communicate with and respond to their constituents better than at any time in history. Consequently, incumbents are very hard to defeat these days, and constituency politics can overwhelm considerations of issues and party philosophy.

Also important today is that, for most legislators, serving in Congress has become a full-time job and a long-term commitment. Unfortunately, this state of affairs sometimes encourages the avoidance of tough votes and controversial issues. Nevertheless, one of the major differences between the early Congress and today's is the legislative productivity of the modern Congress. Whether in education or the environment, national defense or drug abuse, Congress is expected to address the problem and come up with solutions. Fortunately for the nation and for the congressional leadership, most members of Congress are workhorses, not show horses, more eager to get results than attention. Nonetheless, some believe that bringing television cameras into the House and Senate chambers may change this situation in the future. I hope they are wrong.

To Make All Laws clearly identifies the flaws and failings of many of those great and not so great men and women who have served in Congress. This realistic portrait of the personalities who helped make our nation great allows us all to appreciate that our form of democracy is best practiced when the leaders who are elected by the will of the people can reflect people's hopes and aspirations as well as their passions and interests.

Thomas P. O'Neill, Jr.
Speaker of the House, 1977–1986

PREFACE

It is highly appropriate that the Library of Congress commissioned *To Make All Laws,* a history of the Congress by James H. Hutson, chief of the Library's own Manuscript Division. The Library's evolution has followed that of its parent, the national legislature, the branch of American government that is closest to the people.

The Senate and House of Representatives depended on books from the start. In 1789, organized as the First Congress of the United States, the legislators of the new republic secured access to the 4,000 volumes of the New York Society Library, located upstairs from their meeting place in New York's City Hall. In 1791, in Philadelphia, they used the books of the Library Company of Philadelphia. Finally, in 1801, moving to the new Federal City in a swamp south of Georgetown, Maryland, Congress set up a $5,000 fund to buy books "with a suitable apartment for containing them." This was the official beginning of the Library of Congress: books bought in England and housed in the new Capitol.

After the British burned the Capitol (and the Library) during the War of 1812, Thomas Jefferson offered to sell Congress his own 6,487-volume collection, the largest in America, to revive the Library.

He wrote: "I do not know that it contains any branch of science which Congress would wish to exclude from their collection; there is, in fact, no subject to which a member of Congress may not have occasion to refer."

The Senate agreed to pay the appraised value of $23,950, and the House reluctantly followed suit (the entire New England delegation, including Daniel Webster, voted against the idea). Thus was born the idea of a universal library, of use to the legislators, which has proved of increasing use to the nation as a whole.

Congress remained determined to maintain the Library. A Christmas Eve fire in 1851 destroyed more than half of the Library, including many of Mr. Jefferson's books. But Congress replenished the collections and gave the Library its own building in 1897.

Congress has continued to support the Library, and the Library has continued to serve Congress; its Congressional Research Service now answers 500,000 inquiries from the members and staff of the House and Senate each year, with an electronic network speeding communications back and forth. America has been well served by this continuing daily link between legislative action and the treasure house of the world's knowledge. Congress has encouraged the Library to grow and to become the nation's memory, serving scholars, other libraries, and the people as a whole.

The central role of Congress in our nation's history is too little known to most Americans. Enlightening the public about Congress will promote a better understanding and appreciation of our form of government. James H. Hutson's even-handed, highly readable chronicle of Congress's first two hundred years is a good place to begin.

James H. Billington
The Librarian of Congress

THE INSTITUTION AND ITS MEMBERS

☆

The Looking Glass for 1787
Engraving, possibly by Amos Doolittle,
1787
Prints and Photographs Division

Designed by "Trustless Fox," this caricature of conditions in Connecticut in 1787 symbolizes the turmoil and dissention in all the states on the eve of the Constitutional Convention. The ship or, in this case, the cart of state was "deep in the mire." To rescue it was the task of the Framers of the United States Constitution, who gave Congress powers necessary to establish an "energetic" government.

CREATION

"In republican government the legislative authority necessarily predominates." So wrote James Madison in the *Federalist* and so believed the statesmen who helped Madison frame the Constitution of the United States. Congress stands first, in Article 1, in the Constitution. It receives more space than the other two branches of government combined. The Constitution does not specify the number of Supreme Court Justices and it does not name the officers in the President's Cabinet. But when Congress is discussed, no detail is spared: the exact number of House and Senate members is fixed; age and citizenship requirements are stated; individual and institutional conduct is prescribed; privileges are listed; and even salaries are mentioned. The attention lavished on Congress reflected the Framers' respect for the legislative power. It also showed their fear of it.

The Framers feared the legislature because many state legislatures had abused their powers in the disordered times leading up to the Constitutional Convention. Some had cheated creditors by issuing funny money; others had executed criminal suspects without jury trials. To many, the power of republican legislatures for good and for ill seemed irresistible. Everything, Madison worried, might be sucked into the "Legislative vortex." The executive itself was not safe, James Wilson believed, for "the Legislature can at any moment sink it into non-existence."

The Virginia Plan, May 29, 1787
Manuscript Division

Introduced at the Constitutional Convention by Governor Edmund Randolph of Virginia, the Virginia Plan, which reflected the ideas of Randolph's colleague, James Madison, was the blueprint from which the Convention worked to build the Constitution. Article 3 of the plan, proposing that the "national legislature ought to consist of two branches," was adopted without dissent.

The Convention which wrote the Constitution of the United States met, May 25–September 17, 1787, in the Pennsylvania State House, Fifth and Chestnut Streets, Philadelphia.

To tame the legislative power, a bold proposal was introduced into the Virginia Plan, the constitutional blueprint submitted to the Convention on May 29, 1787. Let there be a "council of revision," the plan suggested, composed of the executive and members of the Supreme Court, who would pool their power and authority to counteract Congress. When this idea failed to catch on in the Convention, the Framers relied on a more familiar way to control the legislature: they divided it against itself.

Two branches of the legislature were created: the House of Representatives and the Senate. Being closest to and therefore the "favorite of the people," the House was considered, in Alexander Hamilton's words, to be a "full match if not an overmatch for every other member of the government." How could it be kept from domineering? A "necessary fence" in the form of a Senate was the Convention's solution. Madison thought enough "enlightened citizens" could be found to make the Senate work, but Gouverneur Morris argued that, if the Senate were to succeed as a "checking Branch," it must resemble the British House of Lords. It must, in his view, be elected for life and must have "great personal property; it must have the aristocratic spirit; it must love to lord it thro' pride," an attitude, Morris would be pleased to know, some modern Senates have been accused of displaying. Morris's high-toned ideas were rejected by the majority of the delegates, who believed that a Senate elected at stated periods, containing fewer members than the House, chosen by a different constituency, and serving longer terms would be an effective counterweight to it. "Why," Washington is said to have asked Jefferson in the 1790s, "did you pour that coffee into your saucer?" "To cool it," Jefferson replied. "Even so," said Washington, "we pour legislation into the senatorial saucer to cool it."

Since most state legislatures contained two houses, Americans were comfortable with a bicameral national legislature. Their minds, as George Mason wrote, were "well settled" on this point. But the minds of the Framers were anything but settled about who or what the two branches of the national legislature should represent. With the House of Representatives there was no problem; most of the Convention delegates conceded that its membership should be proportional to the population of the states. The rub came with the Senate, for if it were selected on the same principle, as the Virginia Plan contemplated that it would be, the small states, which had enjoyed parity of representation with the large ones under the Articles of Confederation, would be eclipsed, or perhaps even enslaved by their larger neighbors, as Luther Martin of Maryland feverishly predicted in the Convention. Disagreement between large and small states over representation in the Senate came close to wrecking the Convention, but a solution to the problem was eventually achieved by the "Great Compromise" of July 16, which granted each state equal representation in the Senate and representation proportional to population in the House.

What powers should the Congress, thus constituted, have? More than it enjoyed under the Articles of Confederation was the Convention's short answer. The Confederation Congress had struggled because it could neither

---

The "Great Compromise," July 16, 1787
Manuscript Division

James Madison recorded the details of the "Great Compromise" on a slip of paper which he pasted into his notes on the debates on the federal Constitution. The slip begins with the words, "The whole," and concludes with "an equal vote."

tax nor regulate trade. That the new Congress should have these powers was generally agreed. What else should it be able to do? Here there was no consensus. Even though Edmund Randolph "disclaimed any intention to give indefinite powers to the national Legislature," his Virginia Plan appeared to many to do just that. Madison realized that the delegates would be reassured by an "enumeration and definition" of congressional powers, but he doubted the "practicability" of such a project. The Committee of Detail, however, drew up a list of legislative powers in its August 6 report which, with some revision, was incorporated into the Constitution as the familiar Section 8 of Article 1, which closed with the famous "sweeping clause," granting Congress the authority "To make all Laws which shall be necessary and proper for carrying into Execution" its enumerated powers.

What was the scope of the powers enumerated on August 6? Opinions varied. "Both sides," said James Wilson on August 22, "will agree to the principle and will differ as to its application." Wilson, for example, believed that Congress's power to regulate commerce permitted it to establish "mercantile monopolies," an interpretation that astounded George Mason. But

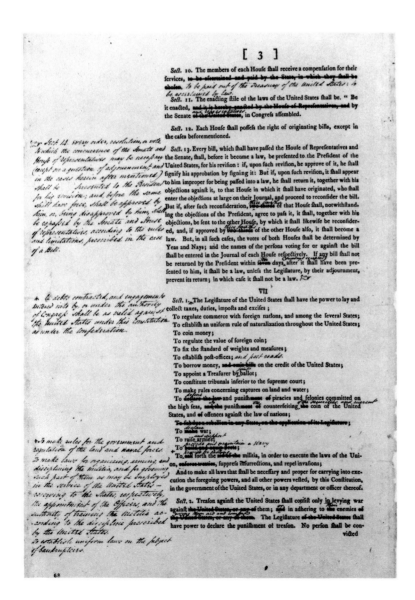

Committee of Detail Report, August 6, 1787
William Samuel Johnson Papers, Manuscript Division

The committee's report, listing and "detailing" the powers of Congress, was printed with wide left-hand margins on which the delegates could enter changes made in the draft Constitution, as the Convention debates proceeded. The report shown here belonged to William Samuel Johnson of Connecticut; marginal notes were made by Convention secretary William Jackson.

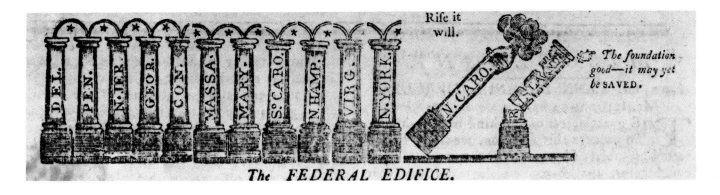

The FEDERAL EDIFICE.

The ratification of the Constitution by the "Eleventh Pillar," New York, is celebrated. North Carolina and Rhode Island did not ratify until after the new government went into operation in 1789.

rather than force disputes about their intentions to an issue, the Framers agreed to disagree about the extent of Congress's powers. Realizing that it was more important to complete the Constitution than to clarify contested issues to everyone's satisfaction, the Convention placed a bet on the future, wagering that the political process would in time produce a satisfactory understanding about congressional powers. That this did not happen, that nineteenth-century Congresses were convulsed by disputes over the extent of their powers vis-a-vis the states, that this issue survived the Civil War and still flickers today, was less a reflection on the Framers than a testimony to the difficulty of deciding on the scope of congressional power.

Adopted by the Convention on September 17, 1787, the Constitution was submitted to the states for ratification. In the ratification contest, extending from the fall of 1787 into the summer of 1788, Congress was one of the many targets of the Antifederalists, as the opponents of the Constitution were called. Equal state representation in the Senate was criticized by Antifederalists in the populous states of Massachusetts and Virginia as denying their fellow citizens their proper weight in the government. The House was attacked with an argument that anticipated modern critics of American politics: too much money was required to obtain and hold public office. The cost of being a Congressman would be so "high," complained New York Antifederalist Melancton Smith, that it would "render the place of a representative not a desirable one to sensible, substantial men who have been used to walking on the plain, frugal paths of life." If the plain, frugal man somehow decided to run for the House, he would find the deck stacked against him, Antifederalists claimed. By making the electoral districts so large and heavily populated—one representative for every thirty thousand people—the system was allegedly rigged in favor of celebrities with broad name identification. The "substantial yeoman" could not afford to compete in such a system and American politics, the Antifederalists charged, would inevitably become the preserve of aristocrats.

Charges such as these had their effect, with the result that the Constitution was ratified with difficulty in the crucial states of New York and Virginia. Nevertheless, by July 1788 eleven states, more than enough to put the government into operation, had ratified. As one of its last acts the Confederation Congress voted that the new Congress of the United States would convene in New York on March 4, 1789.

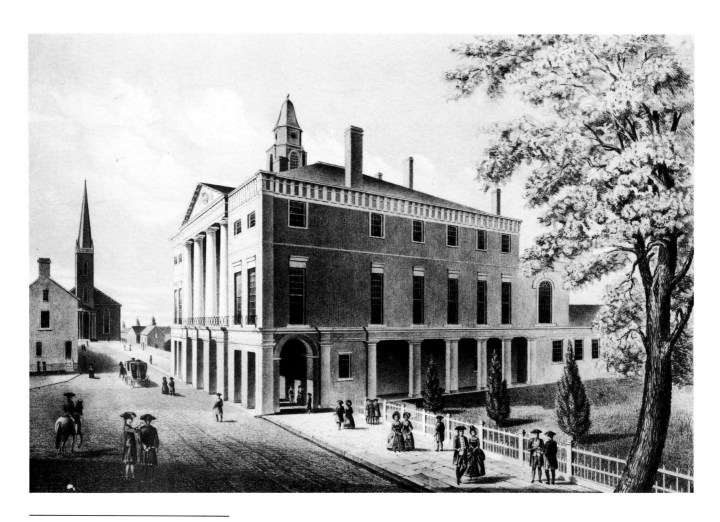

Federal Hall in New York City, 1789
*Lithograph after an engraving
by Cornelius Tiebout
Prints and Photographs Division*

The site of the meeting of the First Federal
Congress in 1789.

LOCATION

☆ ☆

It was the same, yet different. Congressmen arriving in New York on March 4, 1789, discovered that they would be meeting in the same building that the Confederation Congress had used. Yet the structure had been so thoroughly renovated by Pierre Charles L'Enfant, the planner of Washington, D.C., that veterans of the old Congress scarcely recognized it. Congress Hall, as it was called before 1789, had been transformed into Federal Hall, a home fit for a rising people, invigorated by a new Constitution.

A two-story stone structure, Federal Hall stood on Wall Street at the head of Broad Street. The exterior featured four Doric columns on the front side of the second floor, topped by a pediment with a spread eagle. The House chamber on the ground floor was 61 feet by 88 feet and 36 feet high. Members were seated in two semicircular rows with separate desks and chairs. Occupying the second floor of Federal Hall, the Senate was literally an upper house. The dimensions of its chamber, in which the predominant color was crimson, were 40 feet by 36 feet with the ceiling 20 feet from the floor.

The city of New York spent £21,900 renovating Federal Hall, £13,000 of which was raised by a lottery. This costly renovation was a speculation worthy of the building's Wall Street location. Everyone understood that

---

Cong—ss . . . Bound to Conogochegue by Way of Philadelphia
Cartoon, 1790
Prints and Photographs Division

Expressing New York's disappointment at losing the national capital, this cartoon shows the ship of state, enticed by the devil who is summoning "Bobby" (Senator Robert Morris of Pennsylvania), about to plunge to its ruin on its way to Philadelphia. Beyond Philadelphia Congress faces the even more dismal fate of a residence at a blasted wilderness on the Potomac called "Conogochegue." The reference is to Conococheague Creek, which empties into the Potomac at Williamsport, Maryland, just west of present-day Hagerstown; Conococheague was promoted as a site for the national capital in 1790.

Cong.ss Embarked on board the Ship Constitution of America bound to Conogocheque by way of Philadelphia.

The Capitol in 1800
Watercolor by William Birch
Prints and Photographs Division

Congress, the Supreme Court, and the Library of Congress crowded into the north wing of the Capitol—the only part of the building finished—when the government arrived in Washington in the fall of 1800.

New York was to be only a temporary capital, but local authorities gambled that if they provided attractive enough facilities, the government would stay in Manhattan. They failed to reckon, however, with the unshakable determination of Congressmen from the middle and southern states to move the nation's capital farther down the Atlantic coast. On July 16, as a result, Thomas Jefferson believed, of a dinner party deal struck between James Madison, Alexander Hamilton, and himself, or as a result, others suspected, of bribes distributed by the richest man in America, Senator Robert Morris of Pennsylvania, or as a result, scholars believe, of the operation of ordinary, nonconspiratorial political considerations, Congress voted to move to Philadelphia for ten years and then to establish a permanent capital at a site on the Potomac River, a place ridiculed by New Yorkers as a wasteland with an unpronounceable Indian name, Conogocheque. Spurned by Congress, then written off by New Yorkers as a bad investment, Federal Hall fell into decay and was torn down in 1812.

Congress reconvened in Philadelphia on December 6, 1790, in the new Philadelphia County Court House, finished in 1789 at the southeast corner of Sixth and Chestnut Streets. Compared to the well-appointed Federal Hall, the courthouse was, as befitted a Quaker commonwealth, an unpretentious, two-story brick building. In New York Vice President John Adams's Senate desk was three feet above the floor, covered with a canopy of crimson damask; in Philadelphia he made do with a "very plain chair." The dimensions of Congress Hall, as the courthouse soon became known, were approximately 50 feet by 73 feet; the building was lengthened by 26 feet between 1793 and 1795 to accommodate an increasing number of members. As in New York, the House sat on the ground floor, the Senate above it. Like the authorities in New York, Philadelphia officials hoped that the amenities of their town would convince Congress to stay beyond its allotted time, but the members resisted the charms of the Quaker city and in 1800 moved south to what the country's pouting highbrows called the "howling, malarious, wilderness" on the banks of the Potomac.

In Washington only the north wing of the Capitol, designed by William Thornton, was ready to receive the legislators. Thirty-two Senators, 106 Representatives, the Justices of the Supreme Court, and staff of the Library of Congress squeezed into the modest space. The close quarters annoyed those members who were already grumbling about what they considered the barbarous conditions in Washington. We need only "houses, cellars, kitchens, well informed men, amiable women, and other little trifles of this kind

Night Session in the House, 1822
Painting by Samuel F. B. Morse
Courtesy of the Corcoran Gallery of Art

The House met in this space, now called Statuary Hall, from 1807 to 1857.

The Old Senate Chamber
Lithograph after a drawing
by August Kollner, 1848
Courtesy of the Kiplinger Foundation

The Senate met in this chamber from
1810 to 1859.

The House of Representatives, 1866
Lithograph by Sachse
Prints and Photographs Division

An early view of the "modern" House chamber, in use now for more than a century.

to make our city perfect," complained Senator Gouverneur Morris of New York.

In 1801 the House moved into the south wing of the Capitol, into tight, hot, temporary quarters, named the "Oven." When the "Oven" was dismantled in 1804, the members, now sympathetic with the "baked oyster," returned to the north wing. Three years later the House moved into a newly constructed chamber in the south wing, completed under the direction of Benjamin Latrobe. Though the Corinthian columns, carvings, and gallery of the new chamber were a feast to the eyes, its acoustics were so bad that John Randolph of Roanoke pronounced it "handsome and fit for anything but the use intended." A committee was appointed in 1807 to investigate how the "Hall of Congress may be cured of its only defect—difficulty of hearing and speaking in it," but it was unable to suggest a remedy.

During the War of 1812 the British burned the Capitol (August 24, 1814), reducing it to what Latrobe, who was commissioned to rebuild it, called a "most magnificent ruin." Lest the homeless Congress desert Washington, as it had New York and Philadelphia, a group of local citizens, incorporated as the "Capitol Hotel Company," erected a building on the present site of the Supreme Court which they offered to Congress at a low rent until the ruined Capitol was rehabilitated. In this "Brick Capitol"

The Senate, 1895
Composite photograph
Courtesy of the Architect of the Capitol

A favorite of the late nineteenth century, the composite photograph was created by superimposing images, produced earlier, on a scene.

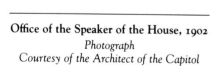

Office of the Speaker of the House, 1902
Photograph
Courtesy of the Architect of the Capitol

David B. Henderson of Iowa, Speaker of the Fifty-seventh Congress (1901–3), used this room.

Congress sat for four years. On December 6, 1819, the original Capitol, now under the supervision of Charles Bulfinch, was ready for use and the Senate and House moved back into their chambers, both of which resplendently exist today. The House chamber, just south of the Rotunda, is now Statuary Hall. The Senate chamber, turned over to the Supreme Court in 1859, has recently been restored to its mid-nineteenth-century appearance, featuring the Vice President's dais, "canopied by crimson drapery . . . held by the talons of an o'er hovering eagle."

By 1850 Congress, comprising 62 Senators and more than 230 Representatives, had outgrown its chambers. In September of that year it voted $100,000 to construct more "ample accommodations" for itself. Extensions were added to both wings of the Capitol, creating the legislative space that exists today. The House moved into the south wing extension on December 16, 1857, and the Senate into the north wing on January 4, 1859.

Most members were pleased with the new space, although one journalist—apparently resolved that something critical must be said about Congress—complained that the flowers on the Senate carpet resembled "gigantic cabbages." Before long, however, the House discovered defects in its ventilation system. So poor was the circulation "that the foul air took on a perceptible cloudy-blue color" and was believed to have caused the deaths from respiratory illness of several members. To correct this problem, a renovation of the House chamber was undertaken in 1901. Another structural flaw produced leaks in the roof around the House and Senate skylights. As early as 1807 Latrobe found the "timbers of the north wing" rotting because of leaks. A major renovation of both chambers in 1949 made them watertight. Modern technology—air conditioning, sound amplification, electronic voting, closed-circuit television—has been installed as it became available. Although the threat of terrorism in recent years has caused sophisticated security systems to be installed in the Capitol, service in Congress was probably more stressful in the decade before the Civil War, when many members wore side arms and were prepared to use them.

Throughout the nineteenth century Congressmen required little space to conduct their affairs. In Lincoln's day, for example, a member "could keep

The 100th Congress: the House
Photograph, 1987
Courtesy of the United States Capitol
Historical Society

The 100th Congress: the Senate
Photograph, 1987
Courtesy of the United States Capitol
Historical Society

all his business in the inside rim of his stovepipe hat." Staffs, if they existed at all, were small. Not until 1885 did the House authorize the use of public funds to pay personal staff members. The Senate, which did not follow suit until 1893, employed only 353 people, including 52 manual laborers and 18 "folders" in 1898. Under no pressure to house staffs, nineteenth-century Congressmen used their desks as offices, although toward the end of the century they began to rent space on Capitol Hill and to work out of committee rooms. House members, however, felt sufficiently inconvenienced by the beginning of the twentieth century that on May 3, 1903, they authorized construction of an office building across the street from the Capitol. The Cannon Building, named for Joseph G. Cannon of Illinois, Speaker of the House (1903–11), was the first of three House buildings erected on the south side of the Capitol. There are also three Senate office buildings on the north side of the Capitol—the first, named for Richard B. Russell of Georgia, was authorized in 1904 and occupied in 1909. Many of the thirty-one thousand men and women employed by Congress in 1988 work in these six office buildings on Capitol Hill.

The Next Senator from New York

Lithograph, The Verdict, *vol. 1*
(1898–99)
General Collections

A view of the alleged control of the Senate by big corporations in the years before the passage of the Seventeenth Amendment (1913). Senator Chauncey Depew of New York is represented as being danced on the strings of tycoons J. P. Morgan and Cornelius Vanderbilt.

ELECTION

Between 1789 and 1987, 11,177 men and women served in Congress— 9,364 in the House, 1,223 in the Senate, and 590 in both chambers. Some were appointed but the vast majority were elected. Article 1 of the Constitution establishes the framework for congressional elections: the House is to be elected by qualified voters in each state, the Senate by state legislatures; members are required to satisfy age and residency requirements; and the states are permitted to regulate congressional elections but Congress may intervene and make its own regulations. This last clause was intended to give Congress the power of self-preservation in case disaffected states tried to wreck the new government by refusing to schedule elections. Antifederalists, however, claimed that it would let Federalists in Congress rig elections by having entire state congressional delegations chosen in seaport strongholds like Boston or Norfolk. Congress might even "make the vote of one gentleman go as far as the votes of a hundred poor men," Patrick Henry charged.

Despite Antifederalist fears, Congress did not intervene in elections. In fact, it left the states with the power of political life and death over individual members. States could change the constituencies of House members by revising suffrage requirements, by "democratizing" them, as they did as the nineteenth century progressed. The abolition of property requirements for the vote, for example, might suddenly produce an expanded electorate, unsympathetic to an incumbent. State legislatures could also alter constituencies by using an early "Massachusetts miracle," the gerrymander. Al-

The Gerry-Mander
Broadside, 1812
Rare Book and Special Collections Division

Coined in 1812, the term *gerrymander* has become a fixture in the vocabulary of American politics. It means partisan manipulation of electoral districts. Local wits identified the Essex County "political monster" sired by the Massachusetts legislature in 1812 as a salamander and dubbed it a gerrymander in honor of its midwife, Governor Elbridge Gerry.

though experts agree that the term should apply to all "discriminatory districting," most Americans associate it with the partisan creation of grotesquely shaped electoral districts. The word was coined in Massachusetts in 1812, when the state legislature created a congressional district in Essex County that resembled, in the opinion of local wits, a dragon or, better still, a salamander. Since the governor of Massachusetts, Elbridge Gerry, was thought to favor the salamander district, it was sarcastically named the gerrymander in his honor. Creative political cartography has flourished in every part of the country. Mississippi devised a "shoestring" district, 500 miles long and 40 miles wide. Other states have crafted districts that observers likened to dumbbells, saddlebags, turkey feet, and frying pans. A House member is most vulnerable to a gerrymander after the decennial census required by the Constitution, for state legislatures may find themselves obliged to redraw district lines to accommodate an increase or decrease in congressional membership. Among noted politicians gerrymandered out of seats were Speaker of the House Galusha Grow in 1862 and Ways and Means chairman William McKinley in 1890.

The Senatorial Round-House
Relief cut, Harper's Weekly, July 10, 1886
Prints and Photographs Division

Unremitting charges that corporations bought state legislatures and dictated the choice of United States Senators helped bring about the passage, in 1913, of the Seventeenth Amendment, requiring the popular election of the Senate. Here the famous cartoonist Thomas Nast depicts the Senate as the mouthpiece of the railroad industry.

Since 1964 the courts have also had the power to change a House district. Eighteen years earlier, in 1946, an Illinois plaintiff, Colegrove, came to the Supreme Court requesting relief from grossly unequal House districts—a rural district of 112,116 and Colegrove's Chicago-area district of 914,053 each elected one member—but the Court declined to enter the "political thicket" of legislative redistricting. The problem did not go away. In 1960 the most populous congressional district contained over a million people, the least populous—Michigan's rural twelfth—177,431. In 1964, therefore, a bolder Supreme Court ruled that House districts must contain substantially equal numbers of voters and required state legislatures to bring districts into conformity with the ruling. To keep his seat today, a Congressman must keep his eye on both the state legislatures and the courts.

Until the passage of the Seventeenth Amendment in 1913, state legislatures elected members of the Senate. Most of these elections went off smoothly enough, but the potential for a fiasco was present from the start, as the New York senatorial election of 1789 demonstrated. Federalists controlled one house of the state legislature, Antifederalists the other. Unable to agree on a candidate, the parties elected no one, leaving their state unrepresented in the Senate for over a year. Congress passed a law in 1866 to eliminate deadlocks in state legislatures, but little improvement resulted. Between 1891 and 1905 there were forty-five deadlocks in twenty states, the most stubborn of which (Delaware, 1895) lasted 114 days and produced 217 votes. During this same period, divided state legislatures left fourteen Senate seats vacant.

Deadlocks degraded American politics. They created the stampeded election at which party bosses produced a last-minute candidate, usually a docile hack, who was elected in a rush to adjourn. They caused riots, as in the Missouri legislature in 1905:

Democrats tried to prevent its [the clock's] being tampered with; and when certain Republicans brought forward a ladder, it was seized and thrown out the window. A fist fight followed, in which many were involved. Desks were torn from the floor and a fusillade of books began. The glass of the clockfront was broken, but the pendulum still persisted in swinging until, in the midst of a yelling mob, one member began throwing ink bottles at the clock, and finally succeeded in breaking the pendulum.

The wire-pulling and horse-trading which, when unsuccessful, caused deadlocks created an atmosphere conducive to corruption. It is easy to exaggerate the venality of post-Civil War state legislatures. Nevertheless, in some states it was a matter for public celebration when Senators were elected "without boodle, booze, or even a cigar." Big business was blamed for buying up the state legislatures, creating the impression among some Americans that "strictly speaking we had no Senate, only a chamber of butlers for industrialists and financiers." This was the theme of the most intemperate indictment of Congress ever written, "The Treason of the Senate" by David Graham Phillips, published by William Randolph Hearst's *Cosmopolitan Magazine* in 1906. "These men of the toga selected by their state legislatures to represent the people," these Senators, Phillips railed, were "the retainers of the money power." In "proving" his charges Phillips indulged in such extravagant exaggeration that fellow muckrakers denounced him for giving their specialty a bad name. His articles, nevertheless, primed public opinion for a proposal that had been gathering ever-widening support: the direct election of United States Senators.

One of the earliest and most persistent advocates of this reform was Andrew Johnson, who introduced direct election amendments in the House in the 1850s and in the Senate in 1860, and who delivered a special presidential message on the subject in 1868. As an alternative, some states tried to bind their legislatures, as they had their presidential electors, to select candidates chosen by popular vote—a procedure that failed in the Lincoln-Douglas campaign in Illinois in 1858—but most reformers eventually agreed that nothing short of a constitutional amendment would purify the process of electing Senators. Five times between 1893 and 1902 the House passed resolutions favoring direct election and each time the Senate pigeonholed them. Prodded by Senator William Borah of Idaho, the Senate finally relented and Congress sent a direct election amendment to the states on May 16, 1912. It was ratified on May 31, 1913. Senate and House members were now both directly elected by voters of their respective states.

What was campaigning for office like in 1913? It resembled politicking at the time of the Civil War more than it did contemporary electioneering. In the earlier eras personal contact and party identification were decisive; television and money had not yet established their dominion over the political process. Money, it is true, has been present in American politics since colonial times. In his first race for a seat in the Virginia House of Burgesses in 1758, George Washington paid £39 6s. to ladle out 160 gallons of election day hospitality to 391 voters of Frederick County—more than a quart and a half of liquor per man. Treating the voters on election day was still in fashion in 1852 when a candidate was sarcastically complimented because:

> He proves to thirsty loafers he's the man
> And drowns their judgment in the flowing can.

An authority asserts that campaign money was first systematically collected by Whig political managers in 1840, because it "cost to build log cabins and to buy hard cider." Running for Congress was, nevertheless, still cheap in the 1840s. According to a friend, Abraham Lincoln claimed that in his House race against a Methodist preacher in 1846 Whig leaders gave him $200. At the end of the successful campaign Lincoln returned $199.25. "I did not need the money," he is reported to have said. "I made the canvass on my own horse, my entertainment being at the houses of friends cost me nothing; and my only outlay was 75 cents for a barrel of cider, which some farmhands insisted I should treat them to."

Abraham Lincoln in 1846
Daguerreotype
Prints and Photographs Division

Lincoln during the year of his successful, seventy-five-cent campaign for a seat in the House of Representatives.

Elect McAdoo, 1932
Photograph
Manuscript Division

Campaigning for Congress had become mechanized by 1932. Depicted is William Gibbs McAdoo's successful California Senate race of that year. Note that the candidate favors the repeal of prohibition.

Canvassing on horseback, by wagon, or by railroad let the candidates woo the voters, a practice frowned on in many parts of America before 1776. James Madison and James Monroe set the pattern for politicking in the new Republic by traveling around central Virginia in the winter of 1789, debating for a seat in the House of Representatives. Voters stood in the snow, listening to them make their pitch. Madison won at the cost of a frostbitten nose, which left lifelong scars. Most early campaigning was not hazardous to the health, although haranguing voters from a stump in a clearing—hence the term *stumping*—required plenty of stamina. Politicians preferred to campaign in towns, where more people could be col-

The torchlight parade was a favorite campaign spectacle from 1860 to 1900. Shown here is a scene from Lincoln's presidential campaign in 1860; candidates for Congress organized similar, if smaller, parades.

Randall for Congress, 1940
*Poster
Manuscript Division*

Posters began to be used extensively in congressional campaigns in the last quarter of the nineteenth century. By 1940, the date of this California poster, the form had evolved to include powerful artwork.

lected. To draw crowds they relied on party workers to organize spectacles with band music, singing, partisan paraphernalia, fireworks, and (a nineteenth-century favorite) the torchlight parade. Since it was impossible to reach into every home with a mailing or a commercial, the nineteenth-century politician relied on party identification to win elections. The individual voter, isolated on a farm or in a hamlet, might not know the candidate, but he would know what his party stood for. The party name could carry the office seeker to victory or defeat.

Despite Will Rogers's quip in the 1930s that "politics has got so expensive it takes a lot of money even to get beat with," the influence of money in political campaigning did not raise a general alarm until it was married to television in the decades after World War II. One expert estimates that the cost of all "election and party politics" jumped from $140 million in 1952 to $1.2 billion in 1980. There are no reliable accounts of the cost of congressional elections until 1970 (over $71 million was spent that year). Figures for presidential elections, though imprecise and unadjusted for inflation, reveal the trend for Congress.

	REPUBLICANS	COST	DEMOCRATS	COST
1912	Taft	$ 1,155,518	Wilson	$ 1,134,848
1948	Dewey	$ 2,127,296	Truman	$ 2,736,334
1980	Reagan	$29,188,858	Carter	$29,352,767

The soaring cost of campaigns has contributed to the weakening of political parties. Unable to meet the financial needs of candidates, parties receive less than absolute loyalty from those who are thrown upon their own resources to raise money and win elections. Weakened parties and indebtedness to private contributors, including political action committees, are developments that trouble observers of Congress and the members themselves. Remedies have been offered since 1910, when a law was passed requiring House members to identify the source of contributions in excess of ten dollars. A number of laws, limiting contributions and requiring disclosure, have been passed since then, four in the 1970s alone. But the ingenuity of donors and the needs of candidates have thus far impeded every attempt to bring runaway campaign spending to heel. The complex history of campaigning for Congress might be summarized as follows: at the beginning low budgets, low party commitment, and hesitant contact with the voters; at midpoint low budgets, high party commitment, and frequent contact with the voters; at present high budgets, decreasing party commitment, and audiovisual contact with the voters.

What kinds of people have been elected to Congress in the past two hundred years? The first Congress was small—at full strength 65 Representatives and 26 Senators—male, white, and descended principally from immigrants from the British Isles, although the first Speaker of the House, Frederick Muhlenberg, was a German-American. Over the years, as Congress grew to its present size (435 Representatives, 100 Senators), its composition changed to reflect the increasing diversity and openness of American society. In the first half of the nineteenth century members like Davy Crockett began arriving from the West, chewing tobacco, whittling, boasting, swearing, and cheerfully flouting society's conventions. Upper-crust Europeans like Tocqueville might sneer at the "vulgarity" these new men introduced in Congress, but the judgment of many foreign commentators suffered from their belief that democracy itself was vulgar.

After the Civil War the big cities began electing the products of their streets to Congress. Tammany Hall, for example, sent a gambler and one-

The Next U.S. Senator
Badge
Manuscript Division

Staples of American politics since before the Civil War, campaign badges and ribbons became ornate and expensive around the turn of the nineteenth century. This gold-tassel-and-lace specimen may have helped Matt Quay win his seat in the Senate from Pennsylvania in 1893.

time heavyweight champion of the world, John Morrissey, to the House in 1867. The doors opened wider in 1870 when the first blacks were elected—Hiram Revels to the Senate from Mississippi and Joseph Rainey to the House from South Carolina. Montana sent the first woman, Jeannette Rankin, to the House in 1917. The first woman appointed to the Senate was Rebecca Felton of Georgia in 1922; ten years later Hattie Caraway of Arkansas became the first woman elected to the Senate. Herman Badillo was the first person born in Puerto Rico to be elected to the House (1970). The twentieth century has, in fact, been a parade of firsts, as members of one ethnic group after another have taken their places in the halls of Congress.

What about the first Americans? Members as diverse as John Randolph of Roanoke, who bragged about being descended from Pocahontas, and the Pennsylvania spoilsman, Matt Quay, have claimed Indian descent. A strong contender for the honor of being the first American Indian member of Congress is Charles Curtis, a Kansan of Kaw-Osage descent, who was elected to the House of Representatives in 1893, served later in the Senate, and, finally, presided over that body as Herbert Hoover's Vice President. However this issue is decided, Americans can congratulate themselves that today it is difficult to identify a group in our society that has not been represented in Congress.

Congressman Davy Crockett
Relief cut, Davy Crockett's Almanack (1838)
Rare Book and Special Collection Division

A symbol of the rough-and-ready frontier, Crockett represented Tennessee in the House of Representatives, 1827–31, 1833–35.

Congressman John Morrissey
Lithograph by Currier & Ives, 1860
Prints and Photographs Division

Heavyweight champion of the world in 1858, Morrissey was every bit as tough as Crockett, but he was a product and symbol of a very different environment—the big cities of the East with their well-oiled political machines. The champ represented New York City in the House of Representatives, 1867–71.

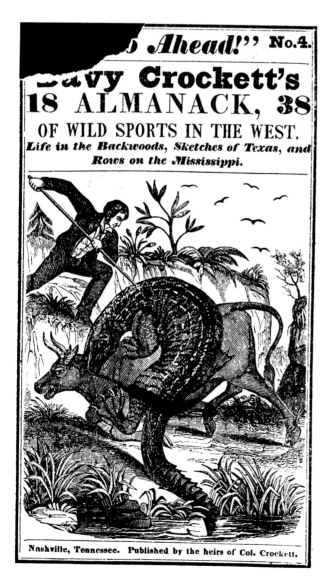

26

Entered according to act of Congress in the year 1872 by Currier & Ives in the Office of the Librarian of Congress at Washington.

ROBERT C. DE LARGE, M.C. of S.Carolina.   JEFFERSON H. LONG, M.C. of Georgia.

U.S. Senator H.R. REVELS, of Mississippi   BENJ. S. TURNER, M.C. of Alabama.   JOSIAH T. WALLS, M.C. of Florida.   JOSEPH H. RAINY, M.C. of S.Carolina.   R. BROWN ELLIOT, M.C. of S.Carolina.

The First Colored Senator and Representatives
Lithograph by Currier & Ives, 1872
Prints and Photographs Division

The Reconstruction legislatures in the Southern states elected these members of Congress and sent other blacks to Washington in the 1870s.

The First Woman Senator
Photograph
Prints and Photographs Division

Rebecca Felton of Georgia, seen here, was appointed to the United States Senate, October 3, 1922, thus becoming the first woman to serve in that body.

One Strike!
Lithograph, Judge, February 22, 1890
General Collections

Shown here is Speaker of the House Thomas Reed bowling over House Democratic opponents labeled "obstructionist," "filibuster," "objector." Reed's ball, titled "firmness," represents the rules he pushed through the House in 1890 to expedite its business. These "Reed Rules" are still the basis of the House rules. Dismayed spectators of Reed's strike are editors of Democratic newspapers and former Democratic Speaker John G. Carlisle. Reed's ally, Representative (later President) William McKinley, looks on with satisfaction.

RULES AND PROCEDURES

☆ ☆ ☆ ☆

The procedures of Congress often puzzle outsiders. "Congress is so strange," said a Russian observing the House in 1947. "A man gets up and makes a speech and says nothing. Nobody listens—and then everybody disagrees." Congressional rules can also be perplexing—mastering them has been compared to learning a foreign language. Some have even charged that the complexity of Congress is conspiratorial, that its procedures have been made deliberately hard to understand to shield it from the prying eyes of the press and public. There is a simple response. Congress is a large institution, handling a multitude of complicated issues, and its ways of doing business reflect the nature of the business it does. It cannot have the simplicity of a town meeting.

As soon as the House and Senate obtained quorums in April 1789, they appointed committees to prepare rules to govern their procedures. Most members of the First Congress, having served in state legislatures or in the Confederation Congress, were accustomed to parliamentary procedure. Whether they agreed with Jefferson's view that even a bad rule was better than none—"it is much more material that there should be a rule to go by than what that rule is"—they knew from experience that without rules they would be lucky to get anything done. The House adopted forty-nine rules grouped under four headings on April 7 and added three more on April 14; the Senate adopted nineteen rules on April 16 and added a twentieth on April 18. Two centuries of making law have, of course, increased the number of rules and precedents in both houses. In 1907 Asher Hinds, clerk at the Speaker's table, published the House's precedents: there were 7,346 of them, filling five volumes covering more than five thousand pages. By 1936 three more volumes of precedents had accumulated and since 1977 eight additional volumes have been issued. The Senate's operations are also complex. By 1981 its precedents filled thirteen hundred pages and it had forty-two standing rules composed of fifteen thousand words compared to the six hundred words required for the 1789 rules.

Members of the first House fretted about its inefficiency. Fisher Ames complained that House rules encouraged the members to "correct spelling, or erase may and insert shall, and quiddle in a manner that provokes me." Thomas Jefferson, presiding over the Senate from 1797 to 1801, was also a critic of the House's rules. In his opinion, the House, like the Confederation Congress, acted in an "unparliamentary" way and its "forms were so awkward and inconvenient that it was impossible sometimes to get at the true sense of the majority." Jefferson thought the Senate was off to a better start and to improve its procedures even more he wrote, while in the chair, *A Manual of Parliamentary Practice*, which was published in 1800. Because he was "rusty" on the subject and could find no research published on it, Jefferson had trouble writing the manual. "So little has the Parliamentary branch of the law been attended to," he wrote a friend, "that I not only found no person here [in Philadelphia], but not even a book to aid me." Jefferson's manual had a curious fate. Though written at his desk in the Senate, it was not officially incorporated into that chamber's rules. The House, on the other hand, decided in 1837 "that the provisions of the Manual should 'govern the House in all cases to which they are applicable and in which they are not inconsistent with the standing rules and orders.'"

The House's action would have pleased Jefferson, who wrote his manual

Thomas Jefferson, draft, "Manual of Parliamentary Practice"
Manuscript Division

Jefferson's manual, published in 1800, is still considered part of the rules of the House of Representatives.

with the hope that it would produce a "conformity" between the rules of the two branches of the legislature. But this did not happen, and as the nineteenth century progressed, the practices of the two bodies diverged. A straw in the wind was the Senate's rejection in its 1806 rules of the "previous question," a tactic used to limit debate. The Senate fully committed itself to unfettered debate in 1841 when it faced a filibuster organized by John C. Calhoun. Derived from *filibustero*, a Spanish adaption of the Dutch word for freebooter, the filibuster, like the gerrymander, has a general and a specific meaning. In its broad sense it means obstruction of a legislature's business by the use—or misuse—of its rules, including roll calls, quorum calls, points of order, and so forth. In its narrow, popular usage filibustering signifies "talking a bill to death," as when an individual and a handful of sympathizers gain the floor and hold it, by making marathon speeches, reading telephone directories, or discussing the virtues of "pot likker" until the patience of the supporters of a bill is exhausted and they give up trying to pass it. Although Calhoun's opponents, the Whigs, controlled the Senate in 1841, they refused to let their leadership cut off debate. The lesson drawn from this episode was that the rules of the Senate would henceforth support unlimited debate on the theory that the minority must not be silenced and that the length of a speech should be governed only by the speaker's sense of propriety. Unlimited debate was now enthroned in the Senate and would reign unchallenged until 1917.

The House turned in a different direction in 1841. Since 1789 it had endured more filibusters than the Senate. The Federalists mastered the practice after becoming a permanent minority in 1800. One leather-lunged stalwart, Barent Gardenier of New York, was challenged and almost killed in a duel in 1808 by a Jeffersonian opponent exasperated by his interminable speeches. A Federalist filibuster might have succeeded in preventing a declaration of war against Britain in 1812 had it not been disrupted by the warhawks' throwing spittoons around the House chamber. Unlimited debate continued after the war, provoking Henry Clay to interrupt one declaimer who purported to be addressing posterity with the remark that "you seem resolved to speak until the arrival of your audience." By 1841 the House had had enough and passed the One Hour Rule, which limited each member to one hour's debate on any particular bill.

Why did the House clamp down on debate? One reason was its size: with over two hundred members by 1840 the House could not allow itself the latitude enjoyed by the smaller Senate. If the individual member was permitted to "range in his native freedom unfettered by any rule," chaos would result and the House would be little better than a "bear garden." A second reason was the Speaker of the House. The Speaker is sometimes compared to the President of the Senate (the Vice President). Both, it is true, preside over their respective chambers, but here the resemblance ends. The President of the Senate is not elected by the membership and frequently belongs to a minority party. Therefore, the Senate has granted that officer little influence over its affairs. One twentieth-century Senate President compared himself to a "man suffering from a cataleptic fit; that he knew everything that was going on; that he could not speak; that he had no responsibility." The Speaker of the House is elected by the majority party and, since Henry Clay's time, has usually been its partisan leader. As such, the Speaker must have the House in an institutional condition to pass a party platform, and its rules must permit action. Thus, nineteenth-century Speakers promoted rules that, in Sam Rayburn's words, would let the House "work its will." They set the House on the road to achieving what was described in 1910 as "semi-military discipline," which enabled it to act as "an efficient legislative factory." But in 1841 these developments were in the future. Steps were taken in that year, however, to differentiate the House and Senate by rules—one set promoting dispatch, the other deliberation.

House leaders in 1841 soon learned what many of their successors discovered: rule changes do not automatically produce the results intended. Legislative rules are arsenals from which everyone can draw and they furnished House conservatives with new weapons as fast as their old ones were shattered. Limit debate on bills? Fine. Then opponents would tie up the House by extending debate on amendments. Reformers countered in 1847 with the Five Minute Rule, which limited debate on amendments to five minutes per speaker. When opponents circumvented this restriction, the House in 1860 prohibited all debate on amendments. Enemies of dispatch then deployed the "disappearing quorum," a refusal of members, though present, to vote. This device they perfected into such a formidable weapon of obstruction that in 1888 the *Washington Post* denounced "the system of rules [in the House] as the prime cause of the wonderful inertia of this unwieldy and self-shackled body."

Within a year a Samson arose who broke the House's shackles—Thomas B. Reed of Maine. Elected Speaker by the Republicans in 1889, Reed stamped out the "disappearing quorum" in 1890 and pushed through other rules that put the House on a fast track. Reed's motto was "the object of a parliamentary body is action, not the stoppage of action." Although he was vilified as a "czar" and a "tyrant" and although his rules, known ever since as the "Reed rules," were denounced with equal vehemence, they were readopted by his Democratic opponents as soon as they gained control of the House. The Reed rules serve to this day as the organizing principle of the House rules.

In the first decade of the twentieth century the tools Reed forged for action were used for reaction by Joseph Cannon of Illinois, elected Speaker by the Republicans in 1903. Cannon, claimed the *Boston Globe*, was "the logical culmination, the odiferous flower of the rules of the House which were established by the first Czar, the late Thomas B. Reed." Although Cannon was lionized by party regulars, his "tyrannical" reign was relentlessly attacked by those who accused him of thwarting the legislative program of Progressivism, a bipartisan reform movement drawing its principal

VOL. LXIV. No. 1648.   PUCK BUILDING, New York, September 30th, 1908.   PRICE TEN CENTS.

"What Fools these Mortals be!"

Puck

Copyright, 1908, by Keppler & Schwarzmann.   Entered at N. Y. P. O. as Second-class Mail Matter.

Our "Abdul the Damned"

Lithgograph, Puck, September 30, 1908
Prints and Photographs Division

Speaker of the House (1903–11) Joseph G. Cannon of Illinois aroused strong emotions. Idolized by his friends, he was condemned as an oriental despot (or worse) by his enemies for his iron-handed control of the House. Here puffing the pipe of "obstruction"—an allusion to Cannon's opposition to Progressive reforms—the potentate is being served by his retainers, House majority leader Sereno Payne and Representative John Dalzell.

strength from his own Republican party. To his enemies Cannon was, literally, a dirty old man. At sixty-seven he was the oldest person ever chosen Speaker. Known as "Foul-Mouthed Joe," he was notoriously profane. He was said to be the tool of the liquor interests, and he was never without a big cigar, which he waved like a scepter. He once invited those attending a meeting—whether in jest or not it was never clear—to "Behold, Mr. Cannon, the Beelzebub of Congress. Gaze on this noble, manly form. Me, Beelzebub! Me, the Czar." The Czar exercised his autocracy through the

House Rules Committee of which he appointed himself chairman (he appointed, in fact, every member of every committee). The Rules Committee decided whether a controversial bill would come to a vote, whether debate would be allowed, and whether amendments would be permitted. So completely did the Speaker control the House rules that in response to a constituent's request for a copy, one member mailed Cannon's picture.

It was in Cannon's Rules Committee citadel that disaffected Progressive Republican House members, led by George Norris of Nebraska, besieged him. Beginning in 1908, the "insurgents" attempted to purge Cannon from the committee. Though failing at first, they were cheered on by constituents who pressed them to keep on "insurging." As the struggle with "Cannonism" continued into the spring of 1910, sensationalists in the press began comparing it to the American Revolution or the "great rebellion of 61–65" as the latest in a series of popular revolts against despotism. On March 19, 1910, the House at last voted on Norris's motion to remove Cannon from the Rules Committee (but not, it should be noted, from the speakership itself) and to make the committee responsive to the House majority. Before a packed chamber, including members of the diplomatic corps, Norris's proposal passed. Beaten but unrepentant, the Speaker pronounced "all the cry over Cannonism . . . a mere bugaboo." In his view someone must

STIRRING STORY WITHOUT WORDS

The Bulldog and the Czar
Cartoon
George Norris Scrapbook,
Manuscript Division

Beginning in 1908, a group of House "insurgents," led by Representative George Norris of Nebraska, attempted to remove Cannon from his citadel in the Rules Committee. By March 1910 they gathered enough strength to succeed in "treeing" the Speaker, purging him from the committee.

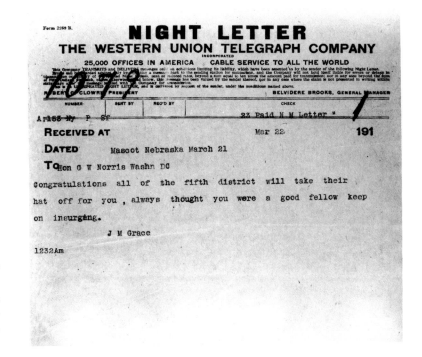

NIGHT LETTER

THE WESTERN UNION TELEGRAPH COMPANY
INCORPORATED
25,000 OFFICES IN AMERICA   CABLE SERVICE TO ALL THE WORLD

ROBERT C. CLOWRY, PRESIDENT   BELVIDERE BROOKS, GENERAL MANAGER

NUMBER	SENT BY	REC'D BY	CHECK
A 155 NY P SF			23 Paid N M Letter

RECEIVED AT   Mar 22   191

DATED   Mascot Nebraska March 21

TO Hon G W Norris Washn DC

Congratulations all of the fifth district will take their
hat off for you , always thought you were a good fellow keep
on insurging.

J M Grace

1232Am

Words from the Home Folks
Night Letter, March 22, 1910
Manuscript Division

During the fight with Cannon, the insurgents were cheered on by constituents who urged them, in the words of a Norris admirer from Mascot, Nebraska, to "keep on insurging."

ROLLIN KIRBY

The Only Adequate Reward
Cartoon by Rollin Kirby, New York World,
March 5, 1917
Rehse Collection, Prints and Photographs
Division

Shown here are Senator Robert La Follette and his "little group of wilful men" being awarded an iron cross by Kaiser Wilhelm for their filibuster against President Wilson's proposal in the spring of 1917 to arm American merchant ships for protection against German submarines. The cartoonist was expressing the sentiments of a large majority of Americans who considered La Follette and his compatriots traitors. Popular outrage against this filibuster prompted the Senate to adopt Rule 22, which gave it the procedural tools, for the first time in its history, to terminate unlimited debate.

Waiting It Out
Photograph, March 11, 1964
Courtesy of the Senate Historical Office

Senator Hugh Scott of Pennsylvania is set-
tling in for the night during the filibuster
against the Civil Rights Act of 1964. The
Senate eventually ended the filibuster, the
first time in its history that it had limited
debate on a civil rights measure.

ride herd on the House and whoever did it would be a lightning rod for
criticism. With the Speaker out of the picture, Cannon predicted that the
Rules Committee "will henceforth bear the odium which has heretofore
been heaped upon me."

Cannon proved to be a prophet. Since his day the Speaker has come
more to resemble, in the words of the House parliamentarian in 1976, a
presiding officer, "judicial and mediating rather than polemical and partisan." The Rules Committee became the House heavy, the target of complaints about high-handedness, although it has, at times, shared the re-
sentment with other committees under imperious chairmen. Some Rules
Committee chairmen have acted like clones of Cannon. Take Philip Camp-
bell of Kentucky, who in 1922 told his committee: "You can go to hell. It
makes no difference what a majority of you decide. If it meets my disap-
proval, it shall not be done; I am the committee; in me reposes absolute
obstructive powers." More polite but no less resolute was "Judge" Howard
Smith, who as chairman of the Rules Committee during the first years of
the Kennedy administration prevented the passage of New Frontier legislation by slipping off to his farm in Virginia and bringing the House to a
standstill. Smith's power was broken in 1961 by the House leadership's ex-
panding membership on his committee to create a hostile majority.

In control of Congress in the 1970s, the Democrats tried to discipline
the committees. They passed rules requiring more "sunshine"—sessions
open to the public, announcement of votes and procedures—and they attacked the seniority system which had produced the Campbells and the
Smiths by electing committee chairmen by secret ballot in the party caucus.
To date, four committee chairmen, three in 1974 and one in 1984, have
been denied reelection.

**Thomas Lloyd's Notes on Debates
in the First Congress**
Manuscript Division

Lloyd was a shorthand reporter who published his stenographic records of debates in the First Congress in 1790 as *Debates of Congress*. From this publication evolved today's *Congressional Record*, one of the means used by Congress to keep the public informed about legislative action.

Lloyd's doodling indicates that he was an unreliable recorder, a fact of considerable importance because his published *Debates*, reprinted later as *Annals of Congress*, is the principal source of information about the intentions of the framers of the Bill of Rights.

In the twentieth century the Senate has moved in the same direction as the House—toward modifying rules that obstruct the will of the majority. The most conspicuous of these rules, unlimited debate, survived until 1917 when it was scuttled by an old friend, Woodrow Wilson. As a college professor Wilson had praised the "Senate's opportunity for open and unrestricted discussion," but the practice looked different to a working politician confronting a national security crisis. To counter German submarines, Wilson in the spring of 1917 asked Congress to arm American merchant ships. His proposal was defeated by a filibuster mounted by Robert La Follette, George Norris, and nine other Senators. Wilson's denunciation of this "little group of wilful men" was temperate compared to epithets of "traitors" and "Iscariots" showered on them by an irate public, one of whom tried to kill La Follette by poisoning his eggnog. Bowing to popular anger at the filibuster, the Senate adopted Rule 22, permitting "cloture," the limitation of debate. As the House had done in 1841, the Senate, under its "cloture" procedure, instituted a one-hour rule for speeches on "measures." It could be invoked by the vote of two-thirds of the Senators present and voting.

Like the House reformers in the 1840s, proponents of cloture discovered that their opponents could thwart them by deft interpretation of the rules. Over the years, for example, Rule 22 was whittled down until it was understood to be inapplicable to procedural questions. This meant that while debate could be limited on "measures," it could not be limited on "motions" that preceded measures, because motions were considered to be procedural. The result, Senator Arthur Vandenberg conceded in 1948, was that "in the final analysis the Senate has no effective cloture rule at all." Not once, in fact, was cloture achieved between 1927 and 1962. But changes in the rules in 1949 and 1959 offered new possibilities, which were realized in 1964 with the first successful application of cloture to a civil rights bill. Assisted by a further liberalization of the rules in 1975, cloture has been achieved sixty-one times since 1964. The struggle with the filibuster took yet another twist, however, with the invention in the 1970s of the "post-cloture" filibuster. Under the leadership of Robert Byrd, the Senate extinguished this innovation in 1979.

Although the rules of the House and Senate are still—and probably always will be—the objects of criticism by pundits and by some members of Congress and although they still furnish resources for obstruction, it is indisputable that they permit more efficient conduct of legislative business now than they did a hundred years ago. The opportunity for the majority to "work its will" is substantially greater in both houses than it was in 1889, when Thomas Reed first began probing the defenses of the disappearing quorum.

Our Congressman—Past and Present
Lithograph, Puck, March 8, 1882
Prints and Photographs Division

The modern Congressman is besieged by petitioners, while his predecessors have the time to declaim about lofty subjects. Usually an unsympathetic commentator on Congress, *Puck* recognized that the pressure of an expectant public, petitioning for favors and constituent services, had changed the nature of life in Congress from the heroic to what often approached drudgery.

Henry Clay Addressing the Senate, 1850
Engraving by Robert Whitechurch
after a drawing by Peter Rothermel, 1855
United States Senate Collection

Clay and his venerable colleagues John C. Calhoun and Daniel Webster, who are shown standing at the far right and sitting at the front left, all delivered memorable speeches on the Compromise of 1850, a complicated series of measures that many hoped would avert civil war.

ON THE FLOOR

☆ ☆ ☆ ☆ ☆

Until the Civil War the floors of Congress were dangerous. Many legislators were armed—during one House debate thirty members pulled guns—and some were prepared to carry their differences to the local dueling grounds. Henry Clay and John Randolph fought with pistols in 1826 and Jonathan Cilley and William Graves with rifles in 1839. The murder of Cilley—for it was nothing less—prompted Congress to pass an act in 1839 outlawing dueling in the District of Columbia. But one statute could not suppress the sectional hatreds, aroused by slavery, which surfaced in Congress in the mid-nineteenth century. The violence that resulted was not the product of an institutional flaw, but of the process of representation itself. An angry society sent angry men to Washington. Sparks flew on the floor of Congress and some of them helped ignite the powder keg of Civil War in 1861.

What has been called "the first and probably the most famous personal encounter on the floor of the House" had nothing to do with slavery or sectionalism, however. Two New Englanders, Matt Lyon, Republican of Vermont, and Roger Griswold, Federalist of Connecticut, were the principals. At issue was Griswold's charge in a House debate in 1798 that during the Revolutionary War Lyon had been forced to wear a wooden sword because of cowardice. Retaliating against his accuser, Lyon spit tobacco juice into Griswold's face on January 30, 1798. Fifteen days later, armed with a "stout hickory stick," Griswold assaulted Lyon as he sat at his House desk. The "spitting hero," as the Federalists called Lyon, managed to get to his

Congressional Pugilists
Engraving, 1798
Prints and Photographs Division

Roger Griswold and Matt Lyon square off in the House in 1798 with a hickory stick and fire tongs as Speaker Jonathan Dayton and assorted colleagues look on.

He in a trice struck Lyon thrice | Who seiz'd the tongs to ease his wrongs, | Congress Hall,
Upon his head, enrag'd fir, | And Griswold thus engag'd fir. | in Philadᵃ Feb. 15. 1798.
| | S E Cor. 6ᵗ & Chesnut fr.

feet and defend himself with a pair of fire tongs before he and Griswold wrestled each other to the House floor. Neither man was hurt and neither was disciplined by the House.

Fists, not tongs or hickory sticks, have been the weapons of choice in the twentieth century. In 1902 "Pitchfork" Ben Tillman and his South Carolina colleague John McLauren were censured for fighting in the Senate. The scholarly Sol Bloom, director general of the U.S. Constitution Sesquicentennial, traded blows with Thomas Blanton of Texas in the House in 1927. There have been other shouting and shoving matches, but perhaps the last real fight on the floor of Congress was a bout between Cleve Bailey of West Virginia and Adam Clayton Powell of New York in the House in 1956. Since then, civility has broken out.

There was a comic opera quality about these twentieth-century tiffs, which, with one exception, was missing from the famous confrontations of the 1850s. The antagonists then meant business. The decade had scarcely begun when Senator Henry "Hangman" Foote of Mississippi (so named because he threatened to hang a New England Senator from the tallest tree in his state) committed the "greatest indignity the Senate had ever suffered" by pulling a loaded revolver on Thomas Hart Benton of Missouri during a debate (April 17) on Henry Clay's version of the Compromise of 1850. The only Senator from a slave-holding state who opposed the expansion of slavery, Benton, who had killed a man in a duel, advanced toward Foote, a veteran of four duels, with the challenge: "Let him fire! Stand out of the way! I have no pistols! I disdain to carry arms! Stand out of the way and let the assassin fire!" Before he could accept Benton's invitation, Foote was disarmed and bloodshed was spared. Six years later another famous episode in the Senate ended less happily for one of the participants.

Charles Sumner of Massachusetts was a fervent antislavery man who by the mid-1850s was spoiling for a fight. At the opening of Congress, December 5, 1855, when "bleeding Kansas" was convulsing the nation, Sumner predicted that "this session will not pass without the Senate Chamber's being the scene of unparalleled outrage." As if to prove himself a prophet, Sumner on May 20, 1856, delivered his famous "Crime against Kansas" speech in which he abused, among others, Senator A. P. Butler of South Carolina as "one of the maddest zealots" who had chosen a mistress who, "though polluted in the eyes of the world, is chaste in his sight—I mean the harlot Slavery." Two days later Butler's nephew, Representative Preston Brooks, entered the Senate chamber to avenge his uncle's honor. Accompanied by another South Carolina Representative, Lawrence M. Keitt, Brooks found Sumner writing letters at his desk and began beating him with a gutta-percha cane, declaiming, in a manner John Wilkes Booth may have imitated, "Let the persons who commit the insult incur the responsibility." Like an offensive lineman, Keitt held off Sumner's would-be rescuers. Unable to rise and defend himself, Sumner was beaten to the ground and was carried from the Senate floor, covered with blood. Although the severity of his injuries was the subject of controversy—Southerners accused him of

political malingering—Sumner did not return to the Senate for over three years. The House, divided over slavery, could not discipline Brooks and Keitt, who were triumphantly reelected by their constituents.

Kansas continued to inflame Congress. In a debate on that unhappy territory in the House in 1858, Keitt, belligerent as ever, called Galusha Grow of Pennsylvania "a black Republican puppy." Yelling that "No Negro-Driver shall crack his whip over me," Grow replied with his fists and a free-for-all erupted. It ended when "Bowie Knife" Potter of Wisconsin grabbed William Barksdale of Mississippi by the head and, finding himself in possession of a handful of hair, discovered that he had pulled off his adversary's wig. "Hurray, boys, I've got his scalp," roared Potter. The brawlers dissolved in laughter, stopped fighting, and shook hands all around.

A House rioting over slavery could hardly be expected to agree speedily on a Speaker. In 1859 two hectic months and forty-four ballots were required to settle on a candidate inoffensive enough to all factions to be put in the chair: William Pennington of New Jersey. A first-time Congressman, Pennington was so ignorant of House rules that he relied on pages for guidance in parliamentary procedure. The Civil War swept him out of office after a single term.

If slavery and the sectional conflict did not produce statesmen great enough to prevent war, they produced speeches memorable enough to be recited by generations of schoolchildren. In the beginning the House was Congress's pulpit, the place where speakers played to the cheers and hisses of the galleries. The Senate did not admit the public until 1795 and might not have done so then had the members not feared that its private meetings were giving the body the reputation of a "'lurking hole' in which conspiracies were hatched against the public interest." Senatorial debates were not an instant hit. In 1806 William Plumer of New Hampshire complained that no one paid attention to the Senate. "We have no stenographers and seldom any hearers in the galleries," said Plumer, who added that "in the other House it was different—galleries are usually attended, frequently crowded, with spectators—always one, often two, stenographers attend, and their speeches are reported in the gazettes."

By 1820 the Senate had become the principal platform for public speaking. One reason for the House's eclipse was the abominable acoustics in its new chamber, occupied in 1807. The One Hour Rule of 1841 further discouraged the art of rhetoric in the House and was criticized on that account by Thomas Hart Benton "as an eminent instance of permanent injury done to free institutions." By 1890 public speaking had been so far sacrificed to legislative efficiency that Thomas Reed declared that the "House of Representatives is no longer a deliberative body." A newspaper reporter in 1931 found the House a rhetorical vacuum: "If ever anything worthwhile is said, few can hear it and fewer still pay any attention." House members themselves, a writer noted in 1963, dismissed the importance of oratory in their proceedings, although they were proud of the clever repartee that could often be heard on the floor.

For the set speech the Senate was the place to be, at least during its "golden age" from 1819 to 1859. Unlike the House, the new Senate chamber, occupied in 1819, had "the advantage of plain walls and few recesses; consequently it [was] a good speaking and hearing room." From 1819 to the Civil War the Senate received men who could put these surroundings to their best advantage, an exceptional group of thinkers and speakers whose talents were magnified by the portentous issues confronting the nation: Calhoun, Webster, Clay, Benton, Douglas, Seward, and many others.

Webster Replying to Hayne
Painting by G. P. A. Healy, 1851
Courtesy of the City of Boston

The debate between Senators Daniel Webster of Massachusetts and Robert Hayne of South Carolina in 1830 about the nature of the Union was one of the great rhetorical exchanges in Senate history. It was the occasion for Webster's famous epigram: "Liberty and Union, now and forever, one and inseparable."

The first of the great speech-spectacles in the Senate was the Webster-Hayne debate of 1830. In an exchange that began over the sale of western lands, Hayne of South Carolina eloquently defended Calhoun's doctrines of state sovereignty and nullification. Webster, who had left Massachusetts with "no disposition to make a speech the whole winter," began fencing with Hayne and then on January 26–27, 1830, delivered a formal speech in defense of the union which became a classic in American political oratory. Public anticipation of Webster's second reply to Hayne, as his speech became known, was high. On the morning of January 26 the stairways of the Senate "were dark with men, who hung to one another like bees." Over "300 ladies with their attendant beaux" crowded the Senate floor. Webster did not disappoint his admirers, concluding with words that were memorized in American schools for generations:

> "Liberty and union, now and forever, one and inseparable."

The death of John Quincy Adams made a deep impression on Americans of his generation. Having been defeated by Andrew Jackson for reelection to the presidency in 1828, Adams retired to Massachusetts. Elected to Congress from the Plymouth district in 1831, he served with distinction for seventeen years before collapsing at his desk with a stroke, February 21, 1848. He died in the Capitol two days later.

Twenty years later events on the Senate floor made an even deeper impression on the public. The sectional controversy had worsened to the point that many Southerners were openly supporting secession. Clay, Webster, Calhoun, all old, all venerated by their followers, all dead within two years, were still in the Senate. In an atmosphere of political Götterdämmerung, they joined together to debate the fate of the Union. On January 29, 1850, the seventy-three-year-old Clay, waving fragments from George Washington's coffin, presented a series of pacifying resolutions that were enacted in September as the "Compromise of 1850." On March 4, Calhoun, dead by month's end, but with defiance still burning in his "piercing, scintillant" eyes, was brought to the Senate floor to hear Senator Mason of Virginia read his last speech, an apology for the South. Three days later Daniel Webster delivered his famous "Seventh of March" speech, supporting Clay's compromise resolutions, which included strengthening the fugitive slave law. Webster was extravagantly praised in some quarters, and just as extravagantly denounced by constituents who accused him of betraying the antislavery cause and insulting the memory of his countryman, John Quincy Adams, whose dramatic death on the floor of the House two years earlier was reverently remembered by Massachusetts abolitionists. Webster, according to an indignant entry in a recently discovered journal of Ralph Waldo Emerson, "chose evil for good."

Webster saw things differently, believing that his rhetoric had pulled the nation back from the brink: "The Union stands firm. Faction, Disunion, and the love of Mischief, are put under, at least for the present and I hope for a long time." He was, of course, wrong, which raises the question of the value of the swelling oratory so beloved by nineteenth-century illustrators and printmakers. The conventional view was stated by Carter Glass of Virginia in the 1930s: "In the twenty-eight years that I have been a member of one or the other branches of Congress, I have never known a speech to change a vote." But if the nineteenth-century speakers did not change votes, they did something more profound: they shaped the nation's consciousness. The Senate before the Civil War was what Theodore Roosevelt called a "bully pulpit." There views of national destiny were articulated which expressed the aspirations of the people in various parts of the country. It would be absurd to claim that soldiers went to war in 1861 with concurrent majority or consolidated government on their lips, but the famous speeches in the Senate, condensed into popular slogans, gave many an average man a sense of the larger issues he was fighting for.

In 1859 the Senate experienced what the House had encountered in 1807: movement to larger quarters with poor acoustics. The topics it considered after the Civil War did not, moreover, inspire public speaking. Who could wax eloquent over civil service reform or tariffs on wool? In addition, Progressive reformers in the early twentieth century popularized the notion that "oratory of the grand style . . . is no longer appropriate to or useful in the discussion of the complicated questions of the day, which call for specialized knowledge." These factors reduced oratory in the Senate to the diminished state it had reached in the House. After World War II speakers in both chambers often addressed empty seats. But, paradoxically, in 1989 the most bashful or tongue-tied member of Congress, rising from his seat for a few remarks, commands an audience far larger than Webster or Clay at the peak of their powers. The reason is that proceedings in both houses are now televised and reach, via cable, homes across the land.

The impact of these large, invisible audiences on Congress is not clear. Certainly, television permits more Americans to watch Congress in action than ever before. Whether these viewers will see a repetition of the high drama and tension that preceded the Civil War is uncertain. Since these theatrics foreshadowed four years of carnage, the tamer tone on the floor of today's Congress should not be disdained; rather it should be welcomed as a sign of the republic's good political health.

CAUCUS CURS in full YELL, or a WAR-WHOOP to saddle on the PEOPLE, a PAPPOOSE PRESIDENT.

PREROGATIVES

☆ ☆ ☆ ☆ ☆

The Constitution establishes certain functions that only Congress can perform, and, to borrow an old term from monarchical governments, these can be called *prerogatives*. It is Congress's prerogative to decide who can become a member. The voters might elect a candidate, but they cannot seat him. The House, for example, refused in 1919–20 to seat Victor Berger, a duly elected Wisconsin Socialist, because he opposed American entry into World War I, and in 1967 it declared vacant the seat of Adam Clayton Powell of New York for alleged high living at the public expense. Anyone familiar with legislative history, going back to John Wilkes's election to Parliament in 1769, could have predicted what would happen next: the constituents of the excluded candidates defiantly reelected them. But these same constituents could reelect their favorites until kingdom come and they still could not be seated until Congress decided in its wisdom (or in Powell's case, in obedience to a court order) to do so.

Another congressional prerogative, confined to the Senate, is advice and consent. No treaty can go into effect without the advice and consent of two-thirds of the Senators present, nor can an ambassador, cabinet member or federal judge be appointed without the advice and consent of a Senate majority. Thousands of appointments have been made and hundreds of treaties ratified using procedures worked out between George Washington and the Senate in the summer of 1789.

On August 22, 1789, Washington, accompanied by Secretary of War Henry Knox, personally appeared in the Senate to advise with it about a treaty with the Southern Indians. The President anticipated a question-and-answer session in which he and his staff would control the agenda. They would put the questions, supply the information, and let the Senate reply. The Senate would be no more than a passive respondent. William Maclay of Pennsylvania recorded his suspicion in his famous journal of proceedings at the First Congress that Washington wished to "tread on the necks of the Senate. . . . He wishes us to see with his eyes and hear with the ears of his Secretary only. The Secretary to advance the premises, the President to draw the conclusions, and to bear down our deliberations with his personal authority and presence."

As an alternative, Maclay reported that he persuaded his colleague and Washington's old friend, Robert Morris, to move that the papers brought by Washington and Knox be submitted to a committee of five Senators who would form their own opinion about the course to be followed. Hearing this motion, Washington "started up in a violent fret" and exclaimed that "this defeats every purpose of my coming here." A committee was appointed, nevertheless, which Washington accepted with "sullen dignity." The President returned to the Senate two days later in better spirits and listened to a

Caucus Curs in Full Yell

Etching and aquatint by James Akin, 1824
Prints and Photographs Division

A towering Gen. Andrew Jackson is circled by a mongrel pack of political opponents in 1824. Jackson was the popular choice for President that year but was defeated by John Quincy Adams when the election was thrown into the House. The "curs" yelping at the general are Adams, Clay, Crawford, and newspapers supporting them.

debate on the treaty. Although displaying a "spirit of accommodation," Washington never returned to participate personally in the advice and consent process. Nor have any of his successors. With its stand on August 22, 1789, the Senate showed that it would bring its independent judgment to bear in advising and consenting and that, fretting presidents notwithstanding, it would be a full partner in the process.

The next congressional prerogative, not exercised in this century, belongs to the House—the duty to select a President if there is a tie vote in the electoral college or if no candidate receives a majority there. On such an occasion Article 2, Section 1, of the Constitution directs the House to break the tie or choose the President "from the five highest on the list" of candidates. Each state delegation in the House casts a single vote and a majority of delegations is required for election. Although "throwing an election into the House" is today considered a political nightmare, the Framers thought that it would be the ordinary means of electing the President—George Mason, for example, believed that Congress would choose the chief executive "nineteen times in twenty."

The first election settled in the House revealed a stunning flaw in the Constitution. In the campaign of 1800 Thomas Jefferson and Aaron Burr were the Democratic-Republican standard-bearers. Although everyone understood that, if elected, Jefferson was to be President and Burr Vice President, the Constitution, unaccountably, did not require the electors to differentiate the President from the Vice President on their ballots (an oversight corrected by the Twelfth Amendment, adopted in 1804). In the process of defeating their Federalist opponents both Jefferson and Burr received seventy-three votes. A tie, according to Article 2, Section 1, was to be broken in the House.

The House began voting on February 11, 1801, and found itself deadlocked because the Federalists mischievously threw their support to Burr: eight states voted for Jefferson, six for Burr, and two were divided. Thirty-five votes followed over the next five days with no change—no state would cast the ninth vote that would elect Jefferson. Against the advice of Alexander Hamilton, who denounced Burr as a "Cataline," certain Federalists began bargaining with him. Loathing Burr less than Jefferson, they offered to elect him President, if he would give them assurances about continuing their pet programs. It has never been clear how far Burr was prepared to go in a scheme that would have subverted the popular will and might have produced civil strife. "The means existed of electing Burr," Representative James Bayard of Delaware told Hamilton on March 8, 1801. "By deceiving one Man (a great Blockhead) and tempting two (not incorruptible) he might have secured a majority of the states." The blockhead and the knaves did not cast their lots with Burr, however, and on a thirty-sixth ballot on February 17, 1801, enough Federalists abstained from voting to give Jefferson ten states and the presidency.

No one expected the election of 1800 to go to the House; everyone expected the election of 1824 would. In that year the contest was between

The Electoral Commission of 1877 in Candlelight Session
Relief cut,
Frank Leslie's Illustrated Newspaper,
March 10, 1877
Prints and Photographs Division

Congress created the Electoral Commission, consisting of five Senators, five members of the House of Representatives, and five Supreme Court Justices, to resolve the disputed Hayes-Tilden presidential election of 1876. The commission's crucial rulings favored the Republican Hayes by a straight eight-to-seven party vote.

candidates with sectional, not national, support. John Quincy Adams was the favorite of New England; William Crawford was the choice of Virginia and Georgia; Andrew Jackson and Henry Clay were the pride of the West and Southwest. The outcome of the election showed that Jackson was the people's choice. He received ninety-nine electoral votes to eighty-four for Adams, forty-one for Crawford, and thirty-seven for Clay. In the states where electors were chosen by popular vote, Jackson defeated Adams 152,901 to 114,023; Clay and Crawford trailed with 47,217 and 46,979 respectively.

No candidate having received a majority in the electoral college, the President must be selected in the House from the top three vote getters (the Twelfth Amendment reduced the field from the top five to the top three). Washington became a bazaar, the scene of nonstop wheeling and dealing. Managers for Adams, Jackson, and Crawford courted anyone who could deliver a vote. Adams won Missouri, represented by a single Congressman, John Scott, by agreeing to keep in office Scott's brother, an Arkansas judge who had recently killed a man in a duel. The Illinois vote, again in the hands of a single Congressman, Daniel Cook, Adams procured with a variety of inducements, one of which was a diplomatic junket to Cuba financed by secret service funds. Henry Clay was a bigger fish. Besides being a Presidential candidate, he was Speaker of the House and controlled the Kentucky and Ohio delegations. Adams landed him with the position of

SAMUEL J. TILDEN—DIED, AUGUST 4th, 1886.

Sagacious, shrewd, and with a heart for Fate,   When, tricked by knavery and despoiled by Might,
Once in his life we well may call him great—   He kept the country's peace—and forfeited his right.

---

secretary of state in his administration. In return, Clay delivered Kentucky, despite the state legislature's instructing its congressional delegation to vote for Jackson, and brought Ohio over to Adams as well. All of this effort would have been wasted had not chance, or, in one participant's view, divine providence, intervened on Adams's behalf. Adams was one vote shy in the New York delegation. As the ballots were being collected from that state's representatives in the House on February 9, 1825, a perplexed Crawford elector, Stephen Van Rensselaer, "dropped his head upon the edge of his desk and made a brief appeal to his Maker for guidance in the matter." When the supplicant opened his eyes, he spied an Adams ballot on the floor and, taking it as a heavenly sign, cast his ballot for Adams, giving him the vote of New York. "In this way it was," Crawford's manager Martin Van Buren complained, "that Mr. Adams was made President."

Adams's election by the House in defiance of the popular preference for Jackson seemed to many to be a mockery of democratic principles. Clay was haunted for the rest of his life by charges that he had delivered the presidency to Adams by a "corrupt bargain," by a deal done, in John Randolph's memorable words, between the "blackleg and the puritan." Some of Jackson's more ardent supporters talked of overturning the result by force, but cooler heads talked them into turning their indignation into the more constructive channel of organizing voters for the rematch with Adams in 1828.

Samuel J. Tilden
Lithograph, Puck, August 11, 1886
Prints and Photographs Division

Many of Tilden's supporters believed he had been cheated out of the presidency by the Electoral Commission of 1877, and some talked of seizing the office by force. Here Tilden is shown declining the burning brand of insurrection. The Electoral Commission observes his patriotic act.

The Hayes-Tilden election of 1876 also left a bad taste in many mouths. The Democratic candidate, Samuel Tilden, was, like Jackson, the people's choice, defeating Hayes in the popular vote by at least 250,000. But competing sets of electors were returned by Florida, South Carolina, Louisiana, and Oregon, and without these states Tilden was one vote short in the electoral college. To decide which set of electors had been properly chosen in the four states, in all of which there was "a great mass of charges of fraud, intimidation, and irregularity," Congress in January 1877 created an Electoral Commission, consisting of five House members, five Senators, and five Supreme Court Justices. By a straight party vote of eight to seven, obtained, it was said, by Republican intimidation of the swing voter, Justice Joseph P. Bradley, the commission resolved every dispute in Hayes's favor, and made him President. Once again there was talk of reversing the result by violence, but the Democrats acquiesced in Hayes's elevation after receiving assurances that Reconstruction in the South would be dismantled and after it became plain that Tilden had no stomach for civil strife. Extolled by his admirers—"tricked by knavery and despoiled by might, he kept the country's peace—and forfeited his right"—Tilden lost some of his luster the next year when a congressional investigation revealed that his emissaries were prepared to buy the South Carolina electors for eighty thousand dollars. While the result was yet uncertain, Hayes wrote in his diary that "all thoughtful people are brought to consider the imperfect machinery provided for electing the President. No doubt we shall, warned by this danger, provide by amendments of the Constitution, or by proper legislation against a recurrence of the danger." To date, we have not done so.

Impeachment is the Congress's most formidable prerogative, "the most powerful weapon in the political armory, short of civil war." By using the impeachment machinery Congress can remove from office any civilian official in the American government—a President, Supreme Court Justice, cabinet member, or one of its own (the first impeachment was brought against Senator William Blount of Tennessee in 1797). The Framers of the Constitution borrowed impeachment from the British just as they were abandoning it (the last impeachment in Parliament was in 1805). In the United States the practice received new life and continues to this hour to be a "terror to evil doers."

Impeachment resembles a legal procedure. The House of Representatives, granted the "sole power of Impeachment" by Article 1, Section 2, of the Constitution, acts like a combined grand jury and district attorney. If it finds sufficient evidence of wrongdoing by an individual brought to its attention, it presents a case against him to the Senate and appoints a team of its members to act as prosecutors. The Senate, which has the "sole power to try all Impeachments," acts as a jury; if two-thirds of its members present are persuaded that the person accused by the House is guilty, he is removed from office.

Since 1789 the House has initiated more than fifty impeachment proceedings, although only twelve cases have been considered by the Senate (another is pending as of this writing). Five convictions have been obtained, all of federal judges. The first casualty was John Pickering of New Hampshire, convicted in 1804 of habitual drunkenness over objections that he was unfit to stand trial because he was insane; the most recent conviction was that of Harry Claiborne in 1986 for income tax evasion. Three impeachment proceedings are landmarks in the history of Congress: those of Supreme Court Justice Samuel Chase in 1805, of President Andrew Johnson in 1868, and of President Richard Nixon in 1974.

The Chase and Johnson proceedings are generally considered to have been abuses of the process because charges were brought by political enemies over political disagreements rather than for the commission of crimes as defined by law. The Jeffersonian Republicans impeached Chase, a bombastic Federalist, for preaching "monarchical principles" from the bench and for arbitrary conduct in court. John Randolph managed the House case before the Senate, a task for which no one could have been more unfit, for he was "illogical to excess and egotistical to the verge of madness." The Senate acquitted Chase in 1805, establishing the principle, some constitutional experts believe, that conviction in impeachment proceedings can only be obtained for an "indictable offense"—an actual crime rather than political antagonism. Andrew Johnson was impeached in 1868, ostensibly for a variety of illegal actions but actually because Radical Republicans in

A High Stakes Game
*Gouache on paper board,
by Jack B. Davis, 1974
Courtesy of Peter Rodino, Jr., Chairman,
House Judiciary Committee, and Jack B.
Davis*

Chairman of the House Judiciary Committee Peter Rodino, Special Prosecutor Leon Jaworski, and President Richard Nixon engaged in a poker game over access to the Watergate tapes. Confronted with articles of impeachment voted by the Rodino Committee, President Nixon resigned his office, August 9, 1974.

the House thought his Reconstruction policy was too soft on the South. The House managers in the Senate, led by Thaddeus Stevens of Pennsylvania, "an old bachelor with a deformed foot and with a bitter tongue," were more competent and vindictive than John Randolph. The Senate acquitted Johnson by a single vote—that of Edmund Ross, whose constituents were outraged by his courageous action: "Kansas repudiates you as she does all perjurers and skunks," was the message from the home folks, who removed Ross from office at the earliest opportunity.

President Richard Nixon's difficulties were caused by the arrest of Republican political operatives for burglarizing the Democratic party's national headquarters at the Watergate Hotel in Washington on June 17, 1972. An investigation of the break-in produced a series of revelations about misconduct in the Nixon administration which led to a bipartisan vote, 410 to 4,

Suggestions for New Dome on the Capitol

Cartoon by Billy Borne,
Asheville Citizen, February 21, 1924
Manuscript Division

The scandal depicted here is the Teapot Dome affair which involved corruption in the leasing to private interests of government oil properties in Wyoming. Senator Thomas Walsh's relentless investigation of the personalities involved, 1923–24, led to a jail term for President Harding's secretary of the interior, Albert Fall.

The "Dough" Boy

Pencil drawing by Harold M. Talburt
La Follette Collection, Manuscript Division

International arms traffickers, the so-called "merchants of death," were believed by some Americans to have been instrumental in drawing the nation into World War I. During 1933–34 both House and Senate committees investigated the influence of the arms and munitions makers on American foreign policy.

in the House on February 6, 1974, charging the Judiciary Committee to establish whether grounds existed to impeach the President. Led by Chairman Peter Rodino, the Judiciary Committee prepared three articles of impeachment, two of which passed in the summer of 1974 by wide margins, 27 to 11 and 28 to 10, and the third by 21 to 17. Faced with the prospect of surrendering tape recordings of evidence of his actions relating to the Watergate burglary, President Nixon resigned on August 9, 1974. On August 20 the House accepted the report of the Judiciary Committee, 412 to 3.

Investigations are one of Congress's most eye-catching activities. From communists to California condors, from merchants of death to the death of merchants, Congress has investigated every conceivable subject over the past two centuries. Yet this high prerogative—the power to conduct an investigation—is not mentioned in the Constitution. No political leader, not even the strictest constructionist, has ever denied, however, that Congress has the right to investigate whatever it pleases. Before 1776 Parliament had the power to investigate, the colonial assemblies and the Confederation Congress had it, and in 1789 it was simply assumed that the power was inherent in legislative bodies. Investigations are justified on the grounds that Congress needs the information they provide to make good laws. They are also defended as a means of increasing the public's information about vital issues. Some politicians relish investigations as a device to embarrass adversaries by putting their dirty linen on public display.

Worse Than a Spanish Inquisition
Lithograph, 1839
Prints and Photographs Division

Secretary of the Treasury Levi Woodbury is being investigated by a House committee in 1839 over the "Swartwout affair," the theft by New York collector of customs Samuel Swartwout of $1.25 million in public funds, with which Swartwout decamped to Europe in 1838. Congress's power to investigate, although not mentioned in the Constitution, has always been assumed to exist as inherent in the nature of a free, parliamentary body.

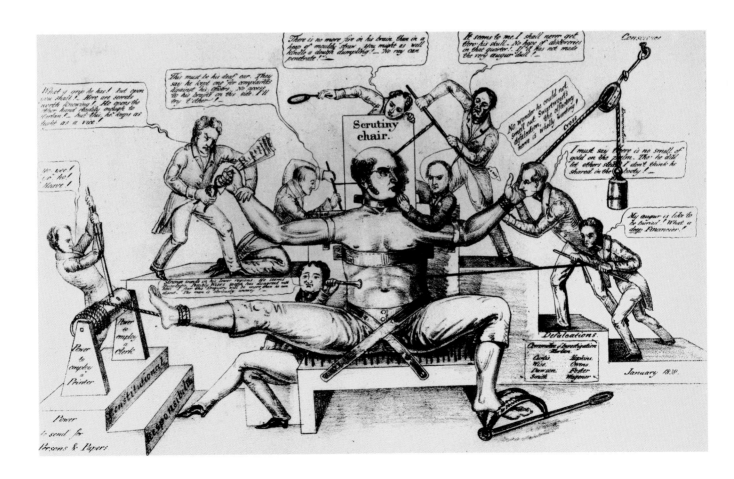

The first congressional investigation was conducted by the House in 1792. Why, it demanded to know, had Gen. Arthur St. Clair's troops been routed by Indians in the Northwest Territory? Defeating a motion that the Washington administration investigate St. Clair, the House undertook the work itself in its capacity as "the grand inquest of the nation." Although 30 investigations had been conducted by 1814, one observer believed that not until the administration of John Quincy Adams did "congressional investigating committees become part of the political machinery of the day." Since that time investigations have multiplied. By 1928 330 had been conducted, and double that number occurred between 1933 and 1958. Since then investigations by committees and subcommittees have become so frequent and so difficult to track (because prior authorization from the congressional leadership need no longer be obtained) that some scholars have stopped counting.

By the early 1950s investigations were in disrepute. Senator Joseph McCarthy's implacable pursuit of communist subversion of the nation's institutions caused a student of the Senate to assert that the "essential dignity of the Institution" had been forfeited. Similar antics by the Committee on Un-American Activities brought obloquy on the House. Still, conditions were not as unprecedented as they seemed. Congressional investigating committees—"smelling committees," Woodrow Wilson called them—were never without detractors, none more intemperate than Walter Lippmann, who in 1922 described investigations as a "legalized atrocity . . . where Congressmen starved of their legitimate food for thought, go on a wild and feverish man-hunt, and do not stop at cannibalism." The exaggerations and fabrications of Senator McCarthy's witnesses did not exceed those of a Washington grocer who testified before the House Judiciary Committee in 1875 that President Grant had seduced his sister by floating into her house at two o'clock in the morning on a cloud. And the bullying of witnesses in the 1950s was nothing compared to the methods used by a House commit-

McCarthy on the Attack
Photograph, 1954
Courtesy of the Senate Historical Office

Senator Joseph McCarthy's investigation of alleged communist penetration of American institutions foundered in 1954 after he attacked the United States Army. Army counsel Joseph Welch here listens incredulously to the Senator's accusations.

Watergate
Photograph, 1973
Courtesy of the Senate Historical Office

Senator Sam Irvin, chairman of the Senate Watergate Committee, strikes a thoughtful pose.

tee investigating the Treasury Department in 1839. Irked by a witness, Representative Balie Peyton of Tennessee, his pistol conspicuous, warned: "He is not to insult me in his answers. If he does, I will take his life on the spot." "You shan't speak," Peyton roared. "You shan't say one word while you are in this room. If you do, I will put you to death." Chairman Henry Wise, also armed, supported his colleague, later recalling that he watched the witness's elbow and "had it moved one inch he had died on the spot. This was my determination."

As a reaction to the controversies generated by Senator McCarthy and the House Un-American Activities Committee, both houses in the mid-1970s adopted rules which gave witnesses many of the procedural protections guaranteed by the Bill of Rights to defendants in courts of law. The result has been to restore the reputation of congressional investigations and public confidence in them and to permit the members to perform the services rendered in the Watergate, Iran-Contra, and other recent investigations. Improvements in procedures in investigations parallel those in impeachment proceedings. In exercising both of these powerful prerogatives the Congress today affords participants fair play and equitable treatment that was often missing in the nineteenth century and up through the mid-twentieth century. Yet the results recently obtained in both investigations and impeachment demonstrate that the revised procedures have been no obstacles to achievements as impressive as any in Congress's history.

MILESTONES

CONGRESS OF THE UNITED STATES.

In the HOUSE *of* REPRESENTATIVES,

Tuesday, the 28th of July, 1789.

MR. VINING, *from the Committee of eleven, to whom it was referred to take the subject of* AMENDMENTS *to the* CONSTITUTION *of the* UNITED STATES, *generally into their confideration, and to report thereupon, made a report, which was read, and is as followeth :*

IN the introductory paragraph before the words, " *We the people,*" add, " Government being intended for the benefit of the people, and the right-" ful eftablifhment thereof being derived from their authority alone."

ART. 1, SEC. 2, PAR. 3—Strike out all between the words, "*direct*" and "*and untilfuch,*" and inftead thereof infert, " After the firft enumeration there fhall " be one reprefentative for every thirty thoufand until the number fhall " amount to one hundred ; after which the proportion fhall be fo regulated " by Congrefs that the number of Reprefentatives fhall never be lefs than " one hundred, nor more than one hundred and feventy-five, but each " State fhall always have at leaft one Reprefentative."

ART. 1, SEC. 6—Between the words "*United States,*" and "*fhall in all cafes,*" ftrike out "*they,*" and infert, " But no law varying the compenfation fhall take " effect until an election of Reprefentatives fhall have intervened. The " members."

ART. 1, SEC. 9—Between PAR. 2 and 3 infert, " No religion fhall be " eftablifhed by law, nor fhall the equal rights of confcience be infringed."

" The freedom of fpeech, and of the prefs, and the right of the people peaceably to affemble and confult for their common good, and to apply to the government for redrefs of grievances, fhall not be infringed."

" A well regulated militia, compofed of the body of the people, being the beft fecurity of a free State, the right of the people to keep and bear arms fhall not be infringed, but no perfon religioufly fcrupulous fhall be com- pelled to bear arms."

" No foldier fhall in time of peace be quartered in any houfe without the confent of the owner, nor in time of war but in a manfer to be pre- fcribed by law."

" No perfon fhall be fubject, except in cafe of impeachment, to more than one trial or one punifhment for the fame offence, nor fhall be compelled to be a witnefs againft himfelf, nor be deprived of life, liberty, or property without due procefs of law ; nor fhall private property be taken for pub- lic ufe without juft compenfation."

" Exceffive bail fhall not be required, nor exceffive fines impofed, nor cruel and unufual punifhments inflicted."

" The right of the people to be fecure in their perfon, houfes, papers and effects, fhall not be violated by warrants iffuing, without probable caufe

RIGHTS
OF THE PEOPLE

On one of its final days (September 12, 1787) the Philadelphia Convention voted, ten states to none, against adding a bill of rights to the Constitution. The delegates were in no mood to deal with so complicated an issue on the eve of adjournment, especially since a bill of rights did not mesh with their theory of government. The Framers considered that the Constitution was created by the sovereign people who gave the government certain limited powers. Since the powers granted did not extend to matters like religion and the press, these areas were off limits to the state. Saying so on paper served no good purpose, for, as Alexander Hamilton argued in *Federalist* 84: "Why declare that things shall not be done which there is no power to do?" Why, in short, have a bill of rights?

Some historians have found the Framers' argument, which became Federalist party dogma, "deeply compelling." Others have ridiculed it, arguing that by the time they considered the bill of rights, their "single-minded purpose of creating an effective national government had exhausted their energies and good sense." Did the Framers actually suffer intellectual burn-out? The American ambassador in Paris, Thomas Jefferson, did not think so, but he was disappointed that they had spurned a bill of rights, which "the people are entitled to against every government on earth." Many average Americans experienced something close to panic when they learned—courtesy of the Antifederalists—that the new government did not explicitly protect their rights. Federalists accused the Antifederalists of unscrupulously frightening these people to promote private ends. Anxieties were especially high among the Baptists in James Madison's Virginia congressional district. To win a seat in the First Congress, Madison was obliged to promise that he would work for a bill of rights when he took his seat in New York, although he privately shared the Federalists' skepticism about the utility of such documents, scoffing at them as toothless, "parchment barriers."

When the House of Representatives convened on April 1, 1789, Madison found little enthusiasm for a bill of rights. According to his Virginia colleague, Richard Bland Lee, some members "objected to recommending any amendments until experience should demonstrate the necessity of them," while others thought the subject "premature" until more "weighty business" such as raising a revenue for the new government was attended to. On June 8 Madison took the initiative and proposed a bill of rights, introducing it with a substantial speech on the subject.

Many Federalists derided Madison's efforts. Some considered him a head-

---

House Committee Report, July 28, 1789
Broadside
Rare Book and Special Collections Division

Produced by a Select Committee of Eleven, this first House report on the Bill of Rights proposed that the components of the bill be inserted into various clauses of the Constitution rather than be added separately at the end of that document. It was at the insistence of Roger Sherman that the Bill of Rights was moved to the end of the Constitution.

line hunter. Promoting a bill of rights, Fisher Ames groused, "may get the mover some popularity which he wishes." Robert Morris thought the Virginia delegate had a case of weak nerves: "Poor Madison got so cursedly frightened in Virginia that I believe he has dreamed of amendments ever since." Madison's specific proposals produced more sneers. Federalists called them "watergruel amendments," "milk and water amendments," and charged that they were placebos, prescribed by Madison for "imaginary ailments." Antifederalists were no kinder, charging that Madison's bill of rights was "whip-syllabub, frothy and full of wind." Madison kept pushing, however, and on July 21 the House appointed a select committee which reported a first draft of the bill of rights to the full House on July 28. The nineteen amendments thus reported were intended by the committee to be inserted at various places in the body of the Constitution rather than to stand separately at the end of the document. The idea of patching up the Constitution in this fashion produced more opposition to the bill of rights. Roger Sherman, for example, protested to the House on August 13 that "we ought not to interweave our propositions into the work itself because it will be destructive of the whole fabric," advice that the House took, although it rejected Sherman's own "detached" bill of rights.

By mid-August, frustrated by the buffeting he had taken over the bill of rights, Madison sounded off at what had become for him a "nauseous project." Yet he persevered and enlisted the support of enough legislators so that on August 24 the House agreed to a package of seventeen amendments and sent it to the Senate. There the bill of rights also had problems. Senator Richard Henry Lee, for example, told a friend that in the upper house "it had been proposed and warmly favored that liberty of speech and of the Press may be struck out, as they only tend to promote licentiousness." So far were these sentiments from prevailing, however, that the House's version of the bill of rights emerged from the Senate condensed, refined, and improved. On September 25 both houses agreed to twelve amendments which were sent to the states by President Washington. By December 1791 the required three-fourths of the states had ratified the ten amendments that are the Bill of Rights.

The credit for the passage of the Bill of Rights goes to James Madison, who can be called the father of the document with at least as much justification as he can be called the father of the Constitution. After some hesitation majorities in both houses of Congress rallied to Madison's cause and bore down the skepticism and opposition of their short-sighted colleagues. The Bill of Rights was Congress's "own," the Washington administration playing no role in conceiving or passing it. On this memorable occasion Congress more than confirmed Justice Brandeis's dictum that the American people "must look to representative assemblies for the protection of their liberties."

But representative assemblies, as the Framers knew, were also capable of trampling on liberties. The fate of the right of petition taught the whole

The Bill of Rights as Sent to the States
Autograph engrossed on vellum, 1789
Rare Book and Special Collections Division

Speaker of the House Frederick Muhlenberg and Vice President John Adams signed the Bill of Rights after it passed both houses of Congress on September 25, 1789. The original Bill of Rights contained twelve amendments to the Constitution. The first and second, dealing respectively with apportionment of representation and congressional pay, were not ratified by the required three-quarters of the states. The other ten amendments went into effect December 15, 1791, when Virginia ratified them.

country this lesson in the 1830s. In 1836, angered by waves of antislavery petitions, Southern members of the House of Representatives, joined by Northern allies, passed a "Gag Rule," forbidding the House to receive such documents. Ex-President John Quincy Adams, now representing the Plymouth district of Massachusetts in the House, immediately began fighting the rule as a despotic measure that deprived Americans of one of their most ancient and fundamental rights. Southern congressmen taunted Adams, who tried to present every petition that found its way to his desk, as a man "who in the course of one revolving moon was poet, fiddler, statesman, and buffoon" and their constituents threatened his life. Mind your business, warned one hothead, or "you will when least expected be shot down in the street or your damned guts will be cut out in the dark." Adams responded

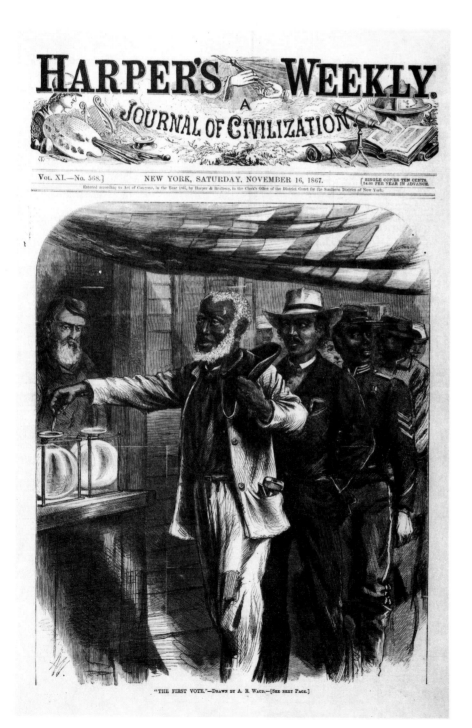

The First Vote
Drawn by Alfred R. Waud, Harper's Weekly, *November 16, 1867*
Prints and Photographs Division

The Reconstruction Acts, passed by Congress in March 1867, paved the way for black suffrage in the states of the Confederacy.

by presenting even more antislavery petitions, some as large as three feet in diameter. In 1842 Southerners tried to persuade the House to censure him but in the view of Representative Richard Thompson of Indiana their leaders were "as unequal to the task of competition with him as would be the timid martin to the proud eagle of the mountains." Overplaying their hand, the Southerners alienated their Northern allies, with the result that the Gag Rule was repealed in 1844 and the right of petition was restored to American citizens.

The fight over the Gag Rule was a skirmish in a campaign that led to the Civil War and the abolition of slavery by the Thirteenth Amendment, in the passage of which Congress enthusiastically joined President Lincoln. Congress and the President disagreed, however, over how the defeated South was to be restored to the Union, a quarrel that Andrew Johnson inherited after Lincoln's assassination. Presidential Reconstruction, as Johnson's program was called, seemed to most Northerners to be too soft on the South, leaving its political culture more or less intact and its blacks more or less in subjection. Relations between President Johnson and Republicans in Congress speedily deteriorated, poisoned by episodes like the interview between Charles Sumner and the President in which the Massachusetts Senator complained that Johnson's tenderness toward the South had "thrown away the fruits of the victory of the Union Army," the President all the while using the Senator's hat as a spittoon.

In December 1865, Republicans established a Joint Committee of Fifteen on Reconstruction (nine members of the House, six of the Senate), led by Sumner and Representative Thaddeus Stevens of Pennsylvania, which helped Congress wrest control of Reconstruction from the President and impose its own program on the country. The Committee of Fifteen rallied public support by releasing reports alleging that the "Black Codes" passed by Southern legislatures legalized a reign of terror in Dixie. One of the most influential of these reports, read in Congress on December 19, 1865, was prepared by Carl Schurz, or "Carl Squirt," as Southerners called him. According to Schurz, "the lash and murder is resorted to to intimidate those whom fear of an awful death alone causes to remain, while patrols, negro dogs, and spies, disguised as Yankees, keep constant guard over those unfortunate people."

The motives of the Radical Republicans who dominated the Committee of Fifteen and guided congressional Reconstruction were a mixture of idealism and self-interest. Stevens, for example, was committed in principle to equal rights for black Americans. "A deep seated prejudice against races has disfigured the human mind for ages," he claimed; equality for blacks "may be unpopular with besotted ignorance. But popular or unpopular, I shall stand by it until I am relieved of this unprofitable labor of earth." Stevens also knew that the Republican party could be relieved of power, if the South reclaimed its prewar preeminence in the Democratic party. Among his papers is a headcount showing a reunited Democratic party winning the 1868 presidential election by thirty electoral votes. Defeat could be averted by making the South Republican, something that could be done by disfranchising white Democrats and enfranchising the blacks who could be expected to adopt the politics of their benefactors. Doing justice to the blacks, including giving them the vote, was thus for Stevens and the architects of congressional Reconstruction both morally right and politically rewarding. Their efforts produced, among other measures, the Civil Rights Act of 1866, which made blacks citizens and conferred upon them a variety of rights, the Fourteenth Amendment, ratified in 1868, which constitutionalized the Civil Rights Act of 1866, and the Fifteenth Amendment, ratified in 1870, which gave blacks the vote. Elections in the fall of 1866 were a referendum on congressional Reconstruction; the verdict, said a leading clergyman, "was an uprising of the people . . . to sustain their own

Voting Projections, 1868 Presidential Elections
Thaddeus Stevens Papers, Manuscript Division

The motives behind Reconstruction were selfish as well as altruistic. This memorandum from the papers of Radical Republican leader Thaddeus Stevens projects the Republican electoral vote in the 1868 presidential elections in the left column at 113. The Democratic vote with the unreconstructed states of the Confederacy included—their vote increased by the necessity of counting blacks at full value rather than at three-fifths—is a winning 143. Eliminating the southern Democratic vote by controlling the Confederate States with newly enfranchised black Republicans would achieve partisan political goals, in addition to humanitarian objectives.

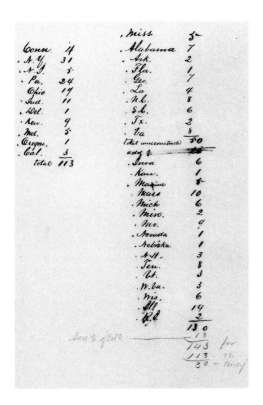

**An Address to the Congress
of the United States**
Pamphlet
Manuscript Division

Carrie Chapman Catt and other women's
suffrage leaders emphasized that the contribution of women to the American effort
in World War I entitled them to the vote,
which they obtained in 1920.

Congress" in its campaign to confer rights on the nation's newest and hum-
blest citizens.

If the hopes of blacks were raised by Reconstruction, the dreams of
women were dashed by it. For their devoted service on the home front
during the Civil War, women's rights leaders expected to be rewarded with
the vote. For the Republican leadership in Congress, however, Reconstruction was the "negro's hour" and his cause could not be jeopardized by asso-
ciating it with an issue as controversial as women's suffrage. Receiving no
satisfaction on Capitol Hill, Elizabeth Cady Stanton tried to keep her followers' spirits up by running for a House seat in 1866, but if her efforts did
not harm the cause—she received, by various estimates, as few as four, as
many as eighty-four votes—the same could not be said of Victoria Wood-
hull's presidential race in 1872 on a platform that included free love, undertaken, she said, with the encouragement of the Greek orator Demosthenes,
who informed her in a seance that "she would be the ruler of her people."

Throughout the 1870s and 1880s Stanton, Susan B. Anthony, and their
Natonal Woman Suffrage Association lobbied Congress. In 1878 Senator
Aaron Sargent of California rewarded their persistence by introducing what

became known as the Anthony Amendment to the Constitution, giving women the vote. Mrs. Stanton testified for the amendment before the Senate Committee on Privileges and Elections, where she was treated with studied contempt by the chairman, Senator Bainbridge Wadleigh of New Hampshire. The Senator's boorishness prevented "the establishment of the faintest magnetic current between the speakers and the committee. It was with difficulty," Mrs. Stanton related, "that I restrained the impulse more than once to hurl my manuscript at his head." In the 1880s both the House and Senate appointed Select Committees on Woman Suffrage, and for a time the legislative tide seemed to be running in the women's favor, but nothing was accomplished until the First World War.

As a result of widespread appreciation for women's contributions to the war effort and despite the picketing of militant females whom some Congressmen denounced as the "Bolsheviki of America," the House voted for women's suffrage on January 10, 1918. The Senate, besieged by counterarguments, ranging from the frivolous—women's suffrage would be "an official endorsement of nagging as a national policy"—to the apocalyptic—enfranchising black women would lead to the "destruction of a large measure of white civilization in the South"—stood out against the Anthony Amendment until June 1919 when it passed it and sent it to the states, where it was ratified, as the Nineteenth Amendment, on August 18, 1920.

What has been called the "modern" civil rights movement came of age

Talking about Rights
Photograph, May 1964
U.S. News & World Report *Collection,*
Prints and Photographs Division

Senate Minority Leader Everett Dirksen and Senator Leverett Saltonstall confer about the Civil Rights Act of 1964. Dirksen and Saltonstall secured the votes of enough of their Republican colleagues to break the filibuster against the act and ensure its passage. President Johnson signed it into law, July 2, 1964.

VOTES FOR WOMEN

THE SPIRIT OF 1776 TO-DAY
"NO TAXATION
WITHOUT REPRESENTATION."
6342

Votes for Women
Manuscript Division

An example of the voluminous literature produced by suffrage organizations lobbying Congress for the right to vote.

Victory for the ERA
Photograph
Manuscript Division

Congresswoman Bella Abzug was a strong supporter of women's issues in the 1970s. Although passed by Congress, the Equal Rights Amendment did not receive the approval of the necessary three-fourths of the states, even though Congress in 1978 extended its ratification deadline for thirty-nine months.

in the 1950s, challenging the nation to make good its promises of equal justice for all. Unlike their post-Civil War predecessors, Presidents in the 1960s took the initiative in proposing legislation to address the concerns of black Americans. They found in Congress a partner in the quest for racial justice—passing the Civil Rights Act of 1964 required, for example, that the Senate for the first time break a filibuster on a civil rights measure. This sweeping act, designed to secure equal access to public accommodations as well as equal employment opportunities, was followed by the Voting Rights Act of 1965 and by the Civil Rights Act of 1968, which complemented the 1964 statute. Throughout the 1960s Congress and the executive worked in tandem for racial justice.

Just as the original women's rights movement was a spin-off of the crusade against slavery, so the campaign for the rights of black Americans in the 1950s and 1960s was a catalyst for a new effort to broaden women's rights. The Equal Rights Amendment to the Constitution, forbidding denial of rights because of sex, was first presented to Congress in 1923. It was introduced, often perfunctorily, every year thereafter until Congress, prodded by an aroused women's movement, passed it in 1972. The amendment did not become law, even though Congress extended the ratification deadline for thirty-nine months in 1978. Congress, an ERA leader exclaimed on this occasion, had shown "the courage of its convictions by not bringing down the curtain on the equality of rights under the law"—a curtain, she might have added, that Congress had raised on American rights in 1789.

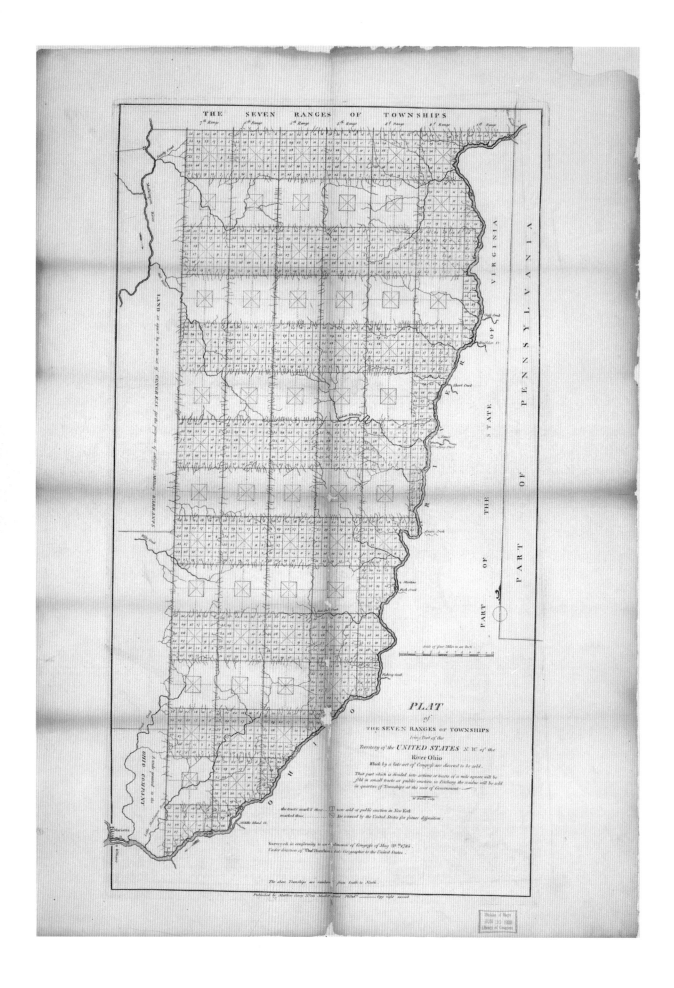

PLAT
of
THE SEVEN RANGES OF TOWNSHIPS
being Part of the
Territory of the UNITED STATES N. W. of the
River Ohio
Which by a late act of Congress are directed to be sold.

That part which is divided into sections or tracts of a mile square will be
sold in small tracts at public auction, in Pittsburg the residue will be sold
in quarters of Townships at the seat of Government.

the tracts mark'd thus ⊠ were sold at public auction in New York
marked thus ⊠ Are reserved by the United States for future disposition

Surveyed in conformity to an Ordinance of Congress of May 20th 1785
Under direction of Thos. Hutchins Esqr. Geographer to the United States.

The above Townships are numbered from South to North.

THE ECONOMY

Twentieth-century Americans regard the management of the economy as the business of the executive. It is the President's job, they believe, to promote economic growth and to keep prices and interest rates low and employment levels high. Although none of these tasks can be accomplished without the cooperation of Congress, the economic spotlight tends to shine more on the White House than on Capitol Hill. In the nineteenth century things were different. Then Congress took the initiative in developing the American economy and the executive remained in the background, except on those occasions when a President picked a fight with Congress by vetoing some favorite economic measure.

Throughout most of the nineteenth century Congress was in the real estate business. For sale were two million square miles of land—the Old Northwest, Alabama, Mississippi, Florida, and the trans-Mississippi West except Texas. Eastern Congressmen, who represented manufacturers fearful that their work force would go West, wanted the land held for appreciation and sold at prices that would discourage migration. Westerners wanted it occupied "in the shortest space of time and under the most favorable auspices." Senator Thomas Hart Benton of Missouri offered the following rationale for quick and easy settlement: "It should be the policy of republics to multiply their freeholders," who would "bring a price above rubies—a race of virtuous and independent laborers, the true supporters of their country." After Jefferson's inauguration the western view prevailed in Congress with the result that terms of purchase were eased as the nineteenth century progressed. As early as 1812 some Congressmen wanted to *give* lands to needy settlers, a policy endorsed by a House committee in 1828. On March 27, 1846, Representative Andrew Johnson of Tennessee introduced a Homestead Bill, authorizing "every poor man in the United States who is the head of a family to enter one hundred and sixty acres of the public domain without money or without price." Denounced by opponents as the "great giveaway," the Homestead Bill was vetoed by James Buchanan in 1860, but Congress repassed it in 1862 and Lincoln signed it. Although Congress modified the country's land policy after the Civil War to meet the requirements of agriculture in the arid regions of the Far West, the Homestead Act of 1862 established forever the principle that the public domain would be accessible to the poor, but ambitious, pioneer.

It took Congress another fifty years to establish a sound system of banking and currency. Congress got the nation off on the right foot by establishing a national bank in 1791. A second national bank, which worked even better, was created in 1816. Andrew Jackson hated this bank for political, not economic reasons (which some doubted he understood). For Jackson,

The Seven Ranges of Townships
Engraving
Geography and Map Division

A 1796 map of seven ranges of townships—each township six miles square—laid out just west of the Ohio River that were to be sold according to acts and ordinances of Congress. The disposition of the public lands was one of Congress's most important nineteenth-century economic activities.

**Set to between Old Hickory and
Bully Nick**

*Engraving, 1834
Prints and Photographs Division*

Andrew Jackson—"Old Hickory"—and
Nicholas Biddle—"Bully Nick"—square
off over Jackson's withdrawal of govern-
ment deposits from the Bank of the United
States in 1833. Biddle's seconds are Long
Harry and Black Dan—Henry Clay and
Daniel Webster—while Jackson is assisted
by Little Van—Martin Van Buren—and
Maj. Jack Downing—a creation of humor-
ist Seba Smith.

the Bank of the United States was a "Monster," "a hydra of corruption," the "germ of an American nobility." Although the Bank's charter did not expire until 1836, Clay and Webster, working together in the Senate, tried to renew it in 1832, hoping to use Jackson's expected veto against him in that fall's presidential campaign. Congress rechartered the Bank, and Jackson, with "all the fury of a chained panther biting the bars of his cage," returned a veto message and rode the veto to victory over Clay in the presidential balloting.

Buoyed by success at the polls, Jackson set out to destroy the Bank. The institution's president, a proper Philadelphian named Nicholas Biddle, resisted, and a fight was on which kept the country's cartoonists working overtime. "Put the screws to him my tulip," effete, port-sipping easterners exhorted Biddle. "Walk into him like a streak of greased lightning through a gooseberry bush," whiskey-drinking westerners urged their hero. Jackson removed the government deposits from the Bank in 1833, thereby sealing its doom. Clay retaliated by persuading the Senate to censure Jackson on March 28, 1834. Led by Senator Benton, working, his opponents claimed,

The Great Tumble Bug of Missouri, Bent-on Rolling His Ball
Engraving, 1837
Prints and Photographs Division

Pictured here is Senator Thomas Hart Benton, as a tumblebug, rolling a ball, titled, Expunging Resolution, toward the Capitol. The reference is to Benton's successful effort in 1837 to delete from the Senate Journal a resolution, adopted in 1834, censuring Andrew Jackson for removing government deposits from the Bank of the United States. The "Black Knights" on the ball are the Senators who supported Benton.

with the persistence of a tumblebug pushing a ball of manure, Old Hickory's supporters rescinded the censure in January 1837 and expunged it from the Senate's Journal.

The destruction of the Second Bank of the United States left a hole in the nation's financial fabric, which was only partially patched by the creation of the National Banking System in 1863. A roller-coaster economy in the years after the panic of 1873 secured a hearing in Congress for currency reformers—to their opponents, monetary dunces—who passed, over executive opposition, bills such as the Bland-Allison Act (1878), a prelude to the panacea offered in 1893 in a stirring House speech by Representative William Jennings Bryan of Nebraska: free and unlimited coinage of silver. Not until the Wilson administration proposed and Congress passed the Federal Reserve Act of 1913 was the nation's currency and banking system given some measure of stability. The Great Depression exposed further fissures in the system and at the request of the Roosevelt administration Congress responded with the Banking Acts of 1933 and 1935; since then, Congress has continued to cooperate with the executive in overseeing the system.

After 1815 the United States enjoyed the benefits of what has been called the transportation revolution. Although Congress cannot take sole credit for this transforming movement—until the 1850s states and localities

Democrats Follow the Fool
Lithograph, Judge, *July 7, 1900*
General Collections

Monetary policy agitated Congress in the years after the Civil War, especially in the 1890s, when William Jennings Bryan led the Democratic party on a crusade for the free coinage of silver at a ratio of sixteen to one to gold. The apostle of free silver is shown here leading a parade of Democratic politicans on what the artist regards as a fool's errand.

Railroad Land Grants, 1878
Geography and Map Division

The shaded areas indicate the lands granted by Congress to encourage railroad construction in the nineteenth century. By 1871 Congress had granted 174 million acres to eighty different railroads.

were major players—it topped it off by tying the Atlantic coast to the Pacific. At first, Congress moved with caution. It financed the construction of the National Road from Cumberland, Maryland, to Wheeling, Virginia, and across the state of Ohio, but recurring doubts about the constitutionality of its actions caused this project to sputter along. Congress had a clearer constitutional conscience about purchasing securities issued by transportation companies. It bought one million dollars worth of stock in the Chesapeake and Ohio Canal Company and offered similar assistance to other canal builders. Andrew Jackson stopped this practice with his Maysville Road veto (1830) but Congress had already devised an alternative strategy to promote transportation: the granting of public lands to help defray the cost of worthwhile projects. This policy blossomed in the 1850s when Senator Stephen Douglas persuaded his colleagues to grant 3.75 million acres to assist the construction of a railroad from Illinois to the Gulf of Mexico.

Congress then went on a railroad-building spree, distributing by 1871 some 174 million acres to eighty different lines. The "Pacific" roads were the principal beneficiaries, the Northern Pacific alone acquiring an area the size of Missouri. Congress also offered loans—sixteen thousand dollars per

VOL. I—NO. 26.   NEW YORK, WEDNESDAY, APRIL 2, 1873.   FIVE CENTS.

THE RIDE TO RUIN.

The Ride to Ruin

Relief cut, Daily Graphic *(New York),*
April 2, 1873
Serial and Government Publications
Division

Initially greeted as a savior by large seg-
ments of the American population, by the
1870s the railroad was seen as a diabolical
force in many parts of the country—the
result of high rates and disregard, in too
many instances, of the public interest.

completed mile—to the Union and Central Pacific Companies. The join-
ing of these two lines with a golden spike at Promontory Point, Utah, May
10, 1869, linking the country coast-to-coast, was hailed as a triumph of
American technology and tenacity. Many considered the railroad builders
a match for the heroes of mythology. "There is more poetry," wrote a Cali-
fornian, "in the rush of a single railroad train across the continent than in
all the gory story of the burning of Troy." But once the public began to be
burned by the greed, arrogance, and dishonesty of too many of the railroad

barons, its attitude changed and some saw the railroad as Jackson did the Bank—as an inhumane, diabolical force in American life. "I find it impossible," said Senator Tom Watson of Georgia, "to refrain from denouncing the manner in which the magnificent blessing of the railroads is sometimes turned into a blasting curse." William Jennings Bryan spoke for the disillusioned when he insisted in 1895 that the title of a railroad funding bill be changed to read: "A bill to amend the eighth commandment that it will read, 'Thou shalt not steal on a small scale.'"

The checkered legacy of federally assisted railroad construction did not stop Congress from supporting new modes of transportation in the twentieth century. Highway acts of 1956, 1958, 1961, and 1962 provided the lion's share of the money to build the interstate highway system, and the Federal Airport Act of 1946 and a subsequent act in 1970 permitted the construction of a nationwide system of jet-age airports. Congress, the record shows, has never backed away from the challenge of moving Americans from place to place.

Neither has it ducked the challenge of protecting American industry. At the request of the House of Representatives, Alexander Hamilton submitted to the members on December 5, 1791, his Report on Manufactures, recommending that industrial enterprises receive the "incitement and patronage of government." As Speaker of the House, 1823–25, Henry Clay packaged Hamiltonian ideas into his "American System"—a program of

The Tribute to the Minotaur
Lithograph, Puck, *December 2, 1885*
Prints and Photographs Division

This free trade cartoon shows a number of states, as young maidens, being sacrificed to the greed of the protected industries of Pennsylvania. Sounding the horn, summoning the monster to consume his prey, is the famous Pennsylvania protectionist Congressman, William "Pig Iron" Kelley. Another Pennsylvania protectionist, Samuel Randall, is steering the boat.

tariff protection and an improved transportation network, over which the products of factory and farm would be exchanged for the benefit of both.

At Clay's urging Congress enacted in 1824 what was generally considered the first protective tariff in American history. Four years later Congress wrote soaring rates into a bill denounced as the "Tariff of Abominations." We are "contending," the Alabama legislature protested, "with an organized body of monopolists, who act in concert, and, like the tiger that has tasted blood, prowls for more with increased voracity."

The appetite of the tiger was kept in check, however, until the Civil War. During that conflict tariff rates were raised to unprecedented heights. After the war the beneficiaries of the high tariff, led in the House by stalwarts such as "Pig Iron" Kelley of Pennsylvania, fought to retain their advantages. And they were successful, because until 1913 rates generally rose, although impartial observers concluded that they should fall. Grover Cleveland unsuccessfully urged lower tariffs on the grounds—strange to modern ears—that the surpluses they were creating were hurting the economy. In 1909 President Taft proposed reduced rates and the House concurred. The Senate, always the bastion of protection, had its own agenda and pursued it with what Henry Cabot Lodge of Massachusetts called "ruthless selfishness." The result, once more, was higher rates. The free list—those items free of duties—was a farce. "Practically ivrything nicessary to existence comes in free," said one wit. "Curling stones, teeth, sea moss, newspaper, nux vomica, Pulu, canary bird seed, divvy divvy, spunk, hog bristles,

---

To Be Sacrificed
Lithograph, Judge, *September 24, 1887*
General Collections

An attack on President Grover Cleveland and, across the arena, Speaker of the House John G. Carlisle, who were working in 1887 to lower the tariff. Lower tariffs, *Judge* believed, would result in American industries and workers being devoured by foreign competitors, foremost among whom was Great Britain.

80

The surplus was considered an economic problem at various points in the nineteenth century. This cartoon blames the surplus on the high tariff.

marshmallows, silk worm eggs, stilts, skeletons, an' leeches. Th' new tariff bill put these familyar commodyties within th' reach iv all." Rates finally fell in 1913 but marched back upward in 1921. The Smoot-Hawley Tariff, passed by Congress in 1930, raised them yet again, to their highest levels in American history. Since this bill was thought to have contributed to the coming of the Great Depression, it gave protectionism, with which Congress had been preoccupied for most of a century, a bad name and dethroned the tariff as a dominant issue in American politics.

Some argue that twentieth-century Congresses have ceded the initiative in economic matters to the executive and to the host of independent agencies, boards, and advisory groups that capture today's headlines. Yet there is scarcely a sector of the modern economy in which Congress has not been active. Consider labor, where measures as diverse as the Child Labor Amendment (1924), the Wagner Act (1935), and the Taft-Hartley Act (1947) all came from Congress. Consider the extensive work of congressional committees overseeing the executive's management of the economy. Or consider Congress's Joint Economic Committee, established by the Employment Act of 1946, or the Congressional Budget Office, which seeks to make Congress competitive with the executive in the access to and interpretation of fiscal data. Clearly, the modern Congress is not about to forfeit its historic role as a major actor in the American economy.

THE ENVIRONMENT

☆ ☆ ☆ ☆ ☆ ☆ ☆ ☆

Environmentalism in the United States came of age at the beginning of the twentieth century as the conservation movement, dedicated to the intelligent use of the nation's natural resources. After World War II the energies of environmentalists shifted to fighting pollution, the multiple poisonings of the country's air, water, and soil. At every stage of its development, environmentalism has had one basic objective: the protection of the world around us from our own greed and thoughtlessness.

Congress took the lead in protecting the environment in the years after the Civil War. In the twentieth century its role has been more complex. Members, frequently from the West, have been accused by conservationists of supporting economic growth at the expense of the environment. Yet some of these same "exploiters" have been the toast of environmentalists on other issues. Take Senator Key Pittman of Nevada. During the Wilson administration he promoted mining legislation that made congressional conservationists like La Follette and Lenroot wince; yet in 1937 he sponsored the Wildlife Restoration Act which enabled the states to set aside millions

Salute to the Environment
Photograph, ca. 1920
Manuscript Division

Senator Key Pittman of Nevada, cosponsor of the Federal Aid in Wildlife Restoration Act of 1937.

Mirror Lake, Yosemite
Photograph by Carleton E. Watkins, 1863
Prints and Photographs Division

Watkins's striking photographs of the Yosemite Valley helped persuade Congress to withdraw the area from the public domain and cede it to the state of California in 1864 as a preservation measure. Congress reclaimed the Yosemite area in 1905, after its exploitation by private interests had become notorious.

of acres for the protection of wildlife and which resulted in the restocking of many species. If environmental issues cut in different ways at different times in Congress, the same can be said for the executive branch. The result is that although some twentieth-century presidents have appeared to be better friends of the environment than Congress, during other administrations the environment appears to have had no friend except Congress.

During the first half of the nineteenth century Congress occasionally passed laws anticipating the modern conservation movement. In 1832, for example, to protect a choice site from mindless exploitation, it withdrew from public sale territory in and around Hot Springs, Arkansas. Congress made no provisions for policing the area, however, and it was soon overrun by squatters and fast buck artists. Fear that a similar fate awaited California's Yosemite Valley spurred Congress in 1864 to pass legislation, introduced by Senator John Conness, to withdraw the valley and the neighboring Mariposa sequoia grove from the public domain and to cede it to the state of California to be administered as an "unalienable" area for "public use, resort, and recreation." Frederick Law Olmsted, the landscape architect, explained in 1865 that it was "in accordance with . . . the duty of republican government that Congress enacted that Yosemite should be held, guarded and managed for the free use of the whole body of the people forever." Congress's duty, according to Olmsted, was to use nature democratically, to prohibit the European practice of private control of scenic wonders. Assuring every American equal access to nature's best would do nothing less than "round out the American revolution," one of conservationism's deep thinkers declared in 1910.

Olmsted identified another motive behind Congress's Yosemite policy as a regard for the therapeutic qualities of nature. Depriving citizens of contact with the outdoors, Olmsted claimed, could cause "mental disability, sometimes taking the severe form of softening of the brain"; it followed that by making nature accessible to all, Congress was practicing preventative medicine on a continental scale. How many Congressmen swallowed Olmsted's nostrums is unknown, but numbers shared his opinion that the first duty of conservation "was the preservation and maintenance as exactly as possible of the natural scenery." Few who saw the first photographs of the spectacular Yellowstone area submitted to Congress in 1872 could have had any other opinion.

From the beginning of the nineteenth century onward, mountain men and trappers had reported subterranean fires, exploding waterspouts, and other fantastic sights on the upper reaches of the Yellowstone River. In 1870 a party, led by ex-Congressman Henry Washburn, set out from Helena, Montana, to explore the area. Its reports spurred Frederick V. Hayden to visit the spot the next summer. A favorite of western boosters because of his theory that "rain follows the plow" (or, that precipitation increases with settlement), Hayden was the leader of one of the four post-Civil War western surveying expeditions, kept in the field by Congress. Photographs by

Yellowstone Falls
Photograph by William Henry Jackson, 1871
Prints and Photographs Division

Submitted to Congress in 1872, Jackson's photographs of the Yellowstone area helped build sentiment for the protection and preservation of the territory as the first national park.

18. GREAT FALLS OF THE YELLOWSTONE

85

his cameraman, William Henry Jackson, and sketches by another member of his party, Thomas Moran, together with reports from the Montanans, convinced Congress that the Yellowstone area was a unique natural resource that demanded to be held in trust for the nation. Consequently, in 1872, it passed an act setting aside two million acres at Yellowstone as a "public park and pleasuring ground for the benefit of the people." The act, barring forever the commercial use of the park's "timber, mineral deposits, natural curiosities or wonders," was a triumph of congressional imagination, providing the "guiding philosophy for all parks that were to follow."

Congress soon discovered, however, that there was a difference between reserving land and preserving it. Poachers, infesting Yellowstone, were on the verge of exterminating its buffalo herds when the park's friends in Congress, including Senator George Vest, who considered it "a great breathing place for the national lungs," rallied to protect it. Conditions were no better at Yosemite, which the *San Francisco Examiner* exposed in 1888 as being run by a "conscienceless crew of vulgar money makers . . . who have turned it into a hay ranch" and who permitted its vegetation to be devoured by droves of "hoofed locusts," as conservationists called the sheep pastured there. Yosemite, it was argued, would be better off under federal control, to which it was returned in 1905. The next year, Representative John Lacey, chairman of the House Public Lands Committee, incensed by the looting of Indian cliff dwellings in the Southwest—vandals were using centuries-old boards for campfires—secured the passage of the Antiquities Act, which permitted the federal government to reserve as national monuments areas of the public domain containing historical landmarks or prehistoric struc-

---

Bull Elk
Photograph by John L. Rogers, 1959
Courtesy of the National Agricultural Library

One of several species restocked as a result of acts of Congress. This picture was taken in the Gallatin National Forest, Montana, in 1959.

Smokey the Bear
Poster, 1962
Courtesy of the National Agricultural Library

Created by the Forest Service, Smokey is one of the most familiar friends of the environment.

...and
PLEASE
make people
more careful!

Only you can prevent forest fires

U.S. Department of Agriculture
Forest Service

NATIONWIDE COOPERATIVE FOREST FIRE PREVENTION CAMPAIGN
SPONSORED AS A PUBLIC SERVICE BY AMERICAN BUSINESS

State Forestry Department

tures. Under this act national monuments were established to protect "caves, forts, canyons, battlefields, birthplaces of famous men, and sand dunes."

By 1915 Washington administered 11 national parks, 18 national monuments, and 2 other reservations, totalling 4.5 million acres. The next year Congress consolidated control over these properties by establishing the National Park Service to administer them. By 1970 sites and land conserved and run by the Park Service numbered 278 units containing 29.5 million acres. There have been occasional fears that Congress would reduce its support for the national parks, but these anxieties have proven groundless. The greatest danger to the parks today is the record tide of visitors swamping them each year.

Proponents of parks wanted them kept as "vignettes of primitive America." Emphasizing preservation put them at odds with the other champions of early twentieth-century conservation, the efficient-use school of Gifford Pinchot and Theodore Roosevelt. In 1891 Congress passed the Forest Reserve Act which permitted the executive to withdraw forests from the public domain. A zealous sequesterer, Theodore Roosevelt also insisted on the rigorous enforcement of the law in the new reserves, a policy that resulted, Oregon's Senator Charles Fulton complained in 1905, in the jailing of the top Republican leadership in his state on charges "ranging from conspiracy to defraud the government to grand theft." Two years later Fulton successfully mounted a campaign in Congress to rescind the President's power to reserve forests, but by that time 175 million acres had been set aside.

Presiding over this realm was the nation's "Chief Forester," Gifford Pinchot. Mocked as the "Sir Galahad of the woodlands," Pinchot believed that

Fish Kill, Ohio
Photograph
Courtesy of the National Agricultural Library

Water is threatened by many sources. These fish were killed by sugar beet wastes.

the essence of conservation was the scientific management of forests to sustain their timber yields, but despite this emphasis on "development" the Forester was too much of a preservationist for westerners like Senator Charles Thomas of Colorado, who complained that his "way to develop was to keep everything petrified and stagnant. To him, so far as his actions are concerned, the American Indian . . . was the ideal conservationist." Men like Senator Thomas would have been dumbfounded could they have seen a fellow westerner, Senator Clinton Anderson of New Mexico, guiding through Congress the Wilderness Act of 1964, which carved a 9.1 million-acre wilderness system out of the national forests and put it off limits to the saw and blasting cap.

By 1920 Pinchot and many of his supporters believed that their basic goals of public ownership and intelligent management of national resources had been accomplished. They welcomed the Mineral Leasing Act of that year as an acceptable accommodation with western interests and would have agreed with Senator Thomas Walsh of Montana that it was one of the most beneficial statutes for his section since the Homestead Act of 1862. Passing on to the 1930s, the country saw a "renaissance" in park conservation, stimulated by the New Deal's Civilian Conservation Corps, and witnessed the "first national awakening" to the necessity of wildlife protection, a movement which began stirring in Congress in 1900 with the passage of the Lacey Act, forbidding the interstate transportation of illegally killed game, and with Representative George Shiras's 1904 bill, protecting migratory game birds.

After World War II priorities in the environmental movement shifted to combating air and water pollution, problems which worsened as the United States grew more urban, more populous, and more affluent. Congress passed a Water Pollution Control Act in 1948, whose grant-making authority it extended in 1956 over the opposition of the Eisenhower administration. In the 1960s Senator Edmund Muskie, "Mr. Clean" to his numerous admirers, emerged as the scourge of polluters. Tirelessly holding hearings on the abuse of the environment, Muskie and his congressional supporters passed a Water Quality Act in 1965 and an Air Quality Act two years later. These acts loosed an avalanche of environmental legislation—the Clean Air Act of 1970, the Clean Water Act of 1972, various amendments to both in 1977, and supplementary statutes covering everything from surface mining runoff to pesticides. The sum total is a body of law complex and, at times, conflicting—the same pollutant, for example, is treated differently under the Clean Water Act and the Safe Drinking Water Act. There is, however, a pattern in modern pollution control legislation. It begins by encouraging state initiatives, introduces federal participation in interstate problems, and almost always concludes with federal "command and control" requirements replacing inadequate state standards. Congress has shown no more indulgence toward environmental dereliction in the executive branch than it has in the states. In the 1980s, aroused by the apparent reluctance of officials in the Environmental Protection Agency to enforce the law and to employ

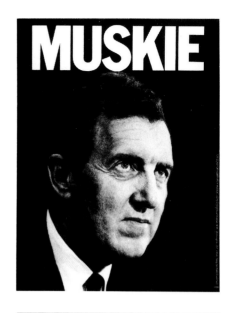

Muskie
Poster, 1968
Yanker Poster Collection
of Propaganda Art,
Prints and Photographs Division

Senator Edmund Muskie was one of the leaders in Congress in the fight for clean air and water in the 1960s.

Father forgive them for they know not what they do.

Father Forgive Them
*Poster, copyright © 1970 by Graphic
Commentary Company
Yanker Poster Collection
of Propaganda Art,
Prints and Photographs Division
Courtesy of Bernard Bloom, Art Director,
and Al Murphy, Photographer*

Many support environmentalism with religious fervor. Notice the imaginative use of
automobile parts.

with becoming zeal the "superfund" to clean up toxic wastes, Congress has issued commands on subjects that "in prior years would have been left to EPA's discretion."

Today's Congress has moved beyond the solicitude for the "dignity of the scenery" that inspired its earliest environmental efforts. Important as that concern was—and is—the stakes of the environmental game have now been raised to the survival of the planet itself and Congress is called upon for resources that would have been inconceivable to the friends of Yellowstone and Yosemite. All of the environmental vision that Congress summoned up in 1872—and more—will be needed in the future.

A Scene on the Frontiers
Drawing
Prints and Photographs Division

The southern and western Congressmen who insisted on war with Great Britain in 1811–12 were called "War Hawks." Among their grievances against the government of George III was the scalping of Americans by Indians, who, the War Hawks believed, were in the pay of the British.

FOREIGN POLICY

☆ ☆ ☆ ☆ ☆ ☆ ☆ ☆

What branch of government should control American foreign policy? The Constitution does not give a clear answer. It gives Congress the power to regulate foreign commerce and to declare war; the executive receives the power to appoint ambassadors and to make treaties, subject to the advice and consent of the Senate. Written into the Constitution though it is, congressional participation in foreign affairs has never sat well with American Presidents, who have claimed preeminence in this area from the beginning. The "transaction of business with foreign nations," Jefferson asserted, "is executive altogether." "Involving Congress in foreign affairs," said a Reagan administration spokesman, "is like having 535 ants sitting on a log floating down a turbulent river—each one thinks he is steering."

Illusory though congressional participation in foreign affairs seemed to this "expert," it was real enough to nineteenth-century Americans who frequently saw Congress steer the country's foreign policy in directions the executive did not want it to go. In fact, the picture that emerges from a survey of Congress's historic role in American foreign policy is not one of fragmented incompetence, so dear to contemporary executive branch apologists, but of a forceful institution that could, and often did, sweep the executive along on a current generated by its own abundant resources.

Congress's first baptism in the fires of foreign affairs occurred in 1795 when President Washington submitted Jay's Treaty to the Senate. Negotiated in London by Chief Justice John Jay, the treaty attempted to solve problems created by the abuse of American neutrality by a British government fighting for its life against revolutionary France. Although the treaty achieved some American objectives—British withdrawal from the Northwest Territory, for example—it was enormously unpopular. Federalists defended it as best they could. Jeffersonian Republicans raged against it: "Damn John Jay," foamed one stalwart. "Damn every one that won't damn John Jay! damn every one that won't put lights in his windows and sit up all night damning John Jay!" The treaty ran a gauntlet in the legislature. The Senate approved it (June 22, 1795) by a bare two-thirds majority, twenty to ten. Usually, the Senate vote on treaties is final, but the House, controlled by Jeffersonians, decided to flex its muscles and kill the treaty by refusing to fund it. After two months of passionate debate, which split friends and families—the first Speaker of the House, Frederick Muhlenberg, was stabbed by his own brother—the House voted by a scant three votes to appropriate the necessary funds.

Jay's Treaty has been defended on the grounds that it bought time for the United States, allowing it to build up strength against the day that it would fight Britain single-handedly. This "opportunity," for so it was viewed by a group of cocky young Representatives from the South and West, came in 1812. Pushed by these belligerent "buckskin statesmen," Congress elected their leader, Henry Clay, Speaker of the House in 1811 and listened to the "War Hawks" thunder away on the floor of the House, urging their fellow citizens to "pull John Bull by the nose." The War Hawks held a particular grudge against the British for encouraging, as they believed, the Indians to ravage the frontiers, allegedly by offering bounties for the scalps of women and children. Their solution to the problem was to expel Britain from North America by taking Canada and, while the country was at it, to kick Spain out of Florida. In 1812 the War Hawks succeeded in seizing control of American foreign policy by bullying the White House wimp, James Madison, into a war with Great Britain. This traditional version of the story now has its critics, but no one doubts the influence of the War Hawks in putting the nation on a collision course with the government of George III.

By ending twenty years of war in Europe, Napoleon's defeat in 1815 freed the United States for a century from the conflicts of the Old World. Congress now turned its attention to its own side of the Atlantic—to Latin America and to territorial expansion in North America. A few members even looked to the Far East. By weakening Spain, the Napoleonic wars fueled the independence movement in her American colonies. Hispanic revolutionaries came to Washington seeking assistance. In response to their

For Their Country's Good
Lithograph, Judge, April 16, 1887
General Collections

The purchase of Alaska, supported by Senator William Gwin of California and other members of Congress, was ridiculed for years after Russia sold it to the United States in 1867. Proposals that the territory be used as a penal colony offend the "original settlers," who want nothing to do with their new neighbors.

pleas Henry Clay, still Speaker of the House, "mounted his South American great horse" and demanded that the cautious Monroe administration help the Latin American freedom fighters. Clay even threatened that the House of Representatives would unilaterally recognize the independence of the new South American republics, since it had the "power to recognize, in the exercise of the Constitutional power to regulate foreign commerce." Before Clay made good on his threat, Monroe in 1822 recognized Argentina, Chile, Colombia, Mexico, and Peru. Twenty years later another campaign by a member of the House, Caleb Cushing of Massachusetts, produced a diplomatic opening to China. Having urged negotiations with the Ta Tsing Empire, Cushing himself was commissioned to conclude the first treaty between the United States and the Chinese government in 1844.

These diplomatic demarches were overshadowed by the emphasis in American foreign policy after 1815 on rounding out the country's "natural boundary." Even in the eighteenth century there were advocates in America of what became known as "Manifest Destiny," the belief that nature and nature's God had decreed that the United States should overspread the North American continent. "Where is it written," a journalist demanded in 1812, "that the American republic should not stretch her limits from the Capes of the Chesapeake to Nootka Sound, from the isthmus of Panama to Hudson Bay?" This conviction enjoyed such widespread support that it would be absurd to claim it exclusively for Congress. It is true, nevertheless, that a proposal to annex Oregon was made in the House of Representatives by John Floyd as early as 1819, but it is just as true that the settlement of the Northwest aroused less interest than events in the Southwest, notably in Texas. The annexation of Texas by treaty in 1844 was overwhelmingly defeated in the Senate, thirty-five to sixteen, because of the perception that it was a proslavery plot, but the Lone Star Republic was admitted to the union the next year by the unprecedented—and some thought unscrupu-

Another Old Woman Tries to Sweep Back the Sea
Cartoon, New York Journal, March 30, 1898
Serial and Government Publications Division

Congress, supported by the people, is about to overwhelm President William McKinley, who is trying to sweep back the popular tide demanding war with Spain.

lous—use of a joint resolution of Congress, bringing cries of "Diabolism Triumphant" from the enemies of slavery. The war with Mexico, which followed annexation, produced notable dissenting speeches by Representatives Abraham Lincoln, David Wilmot, and others; its successful conclusion brought the United States Texas, California, and the lands between.

The extension of the Republic to the West Coast did not satisfy some congressional appetites. At the end of 1859, for example, Senator William Gwin of California approached the Russian ambassador to Washington, Baron Stoeckl, with an offer to buy Alaska. Though ridiculed as a frozen wasteland fit only for a penal colony where prisoners and polar bears would uneasily coexist, Alaska, purchased for a pittance in 1867, is now recognized as a masterstroke of American foreign policy.

Not so the country's flirtation with Cuba, whose acquisition had been anticipated as early as Thomas Jefferson's administration. "It is our destiny," declared Senator Stephen Douglas in 1858, "to have Cuba and it is folly to debate the question. It naturally belongs to the American Continent." A revolt against Spanish rule, which erupted on the island in 1895, was front-page news in the United States. Public opinion, whipped up by a sensationalist press, backed the revolutionaries and soon demanded that Congress declare war against the Spanish "oppressors." Every member "had two or three newspapers in his district—most of them printed in red ink and shouting for blood," a Representative from Maine later recalled.

The President at the time, William McKinley, had a healthy respect for the power of Congress in foreign affairs, because soon after his inauguration the Senate had defeated an Anglo-American arbitration treaty (May 5, 1897) which he strongly supported. The Senate had, in fact, approved no major treaty since 1871, an intransigence that required the executive, in Woodrow Wilson's opinion, to "approach that body as a servant conferring with a master and of course deferring to that master." Although McKinley personally opposed war with Spain—and was accordingly denounced as a "white livered cur" by leaders of his party—and although he could have settled the Cuban problem by quiet diplomacy, he turned it over to Congress, knowing that it would declare war, which it did (April 25, 1898). Some scholars have assailed McKinley for caving into Congress, but others have cited congressional control of foreign affairs as a justification for his action: Congress "would have declared war on its own account, overridden his veto, and left him a newly elected but early repudiated president."

The war with Spain, quick and successful, made the United States the master of her enemy's overseas empire, which included the Philippines. According to one wag, most Americans did not know whether "they were islands or canned goods," and among this benighted number was the President, who confessed that, when informed that Americans had captured the Philippines, he "could not have told where those darned islands were within 2,000 miles." A group of Senators, led by George Frisbie Hoar of Massachusetts, warned that by keeping the islands, the United States would be for-

The Expansion Beverage
Lithography, Judge, *February 3, 1900*
General Collections

The label on the beverage depicts Senator Albert Beveridge of Indiana whose Senate speech of January 9, 1900, supporting annexation of the Philippines, is quoted in the upper left corner. Like new wine in old bottles, Beveridge's speech shatters the brittle mug of Senator George Hoar, a leading anti-imperialist spokesman, who is sent sprawling on the floor of the Senate.

The Real Meaning of Imperialism
Lithograph, Verdict, *December 26, 1898*
General Collections

The chariot of imperialism, driven by Senator Mark Hanna and pushed by John Bull—the British government—enters the Senate, crushing American traditions embodied in the Constitution and the Monroe Doctrine. President William McKinley, chained as a captive to Hanna's chariot, trails along behind it.

THE EXPANSION BEVERAGE THAT MADE SENATOR HOAR LOOK LIKE THIRTY CENTS.

WAKE ME UP WHEN THE WAR IS OVER.

swearing its heritage and following dictators and tyrants into the atrocities and immoralities of imperialism, but they failed by a narrow margin to prevent the ratification of an annexation treaty on February 6, 1899. Although members of Congress and their anti-imperialist allies tried to reverse this decision, they were thwarted by the political skills and eloquence of men like Senator Albert Beveridge of Indiana, and the United States retained the Philippines until after World War II.

In the American system of government wars have tilted the balance of power toward the executive, who is commander-in-chief of the nation's armed forces. It was not surprising, then, that during World War I Woodrow Wilson was riding high. Power went to his head, some believe, causing him to snub the Senate during the peace negotiations of 1919, although he had earlier vowed to be "less stiff and offish" toward that body. The result was the most searing foreign policy controversy since Jay's Treaty. The Republican Senate, led by Henry Cabot Lodge of Massachusetts, refused to approve the Treaty of Versailles without reservations and Wilson refused to compromise with his opponents. As a result, the Senate rejected the treaty and with it American participation in the League of Nations, to Lodge and his associates "the evil thing with a holy name." Wilson's defeat led Congress to seize the "guiding reins of foreign policy in the years 1919 to 1939." At the initiative of Senator William Borah, using the appropriations power, Congress forced President Harding to consent to the Washington Conference of 1922, called to limit naval armaments. During those decades the Senate consistently rebuffed executive efforts to bring the United States

A Bipartisan Team
Photograph, 1948
Courtesy of the Senate Historical Office

Senators Tom Connally (*left*) and Arthur Vandenberg were architects of bipartisanship in foreign affairs in the 1940s.

"I Haven't Run into Anything like This"
Cartoon by Herblock, Washington Post,
November 8, 1973
Copyright © 1973 by Herblock

Toward the end of the Vietnam War Congress began to assert its power in foreign affairs. Here President Nixon's veto of the War Powers Bill is overridden by Congress's heavier armor.

into the World Court. And even though Congress granted Franklin Roosevelt unprecedented power to deal with the domestic crises of the 1930s, it kept him on a short leash in foreign affairs by passing the Neutrality Acts of 1935 and 1937 which limited executive discretion in dealing with developments in Europe.

During World War II the executive, again, dominated the American government. After the war, Congress, having no appetite for another Wilson-style bloodletting, opted for bipartisanship, a policy of cooperation with the executive in foreign affairs. Notable practitioners of this policy were Republican Senator Arthur Vandenberg, who stoutly supported President Truman, and Democratic Senator Lyndon Johnson, who rallied his forces behind President Eisenhower. According to Johnson, "partisanship in foreign affairs would place a loaded gun at the President's temple . . . in our dealings with other nations, only one man can speak for our country. He cannot speak clearly if his words must be strained through a Congressional gag."

Having become accustomed to executive leadership in foreign policy in the post-World War II period, some Americans considered it improper and perhaps even unpatriotic when Congress began aggressively reasserting its influence in world affairs toward the end of the Vietnam War. The War Powers Act of 1973 (passed over a presidential veto) sought to impose a congressional check on the executive's commitment of American troops abroad; the Foreign Military Sales Act of 1974 sought the same result on arms sales to foreign nations. Continuing its activism in foreign policy, Congress in 1988 scuttled the administration's Central American policy by refusing to fund the Nicaraguan contras. Historically, there was nothing unusual about Congress's assertiveness in foreign affairs; what was uncharacteristic was congressional deference to the executive after World War II under the banner of bipartisanship. There can be arguments about which of these postures has served the national interest better, but there can be no argument that for most of our history Congress has been an active and, at times, dominant player in foreign policy.

Little Red Schoolhouse

Alabama township plat, 1822
Courtesy of the Cartographic Branch,
National Archives and Records
Administration

Congress's promotion of knowledge began as early as the Land Ordinance of 1785 in which the Confederation Congress required townships to set aside one section to support a public school. In this Alabama plat of 1822 the school appears front and center.

THE PROMOTION
OF KNOWLEDGE

Congress was promoting education in the United States before the executive and judicial branches of government existed. Under the Articles of Confederation Congress passed the Land Ordinance of 1785, requiring every township in the Northwest Territory to set aside one section "for the maintenance of public schools." Using the public lands to promote knowledge was a masterstroke which gave Congress the means, in the nineteenth century, to create an educational marvel, a nationwide system of publicly financed higher education.

Between 1789 and 1857 Congress donated more than 67 million acres to states and territories to support various educational projects. This was not good enough for Representative Justin Morrill of Vermont, who on December 14, 1857, introduced in the House a "Bill Granting Lands for Agricultural Colleges." Morrill was worried by the apparent "degenerate and

Justin Smith Morrill
Photograph
Prints and Photographs Division

Congressman and Senator from Vermont, Morrill was one of the great patrons of learning in congressional history.

Speech on the Land Grant College Bill
Pamphlet, 1858
Manuscript Division

Morrill's greatest contribution to the pro-
motion of knowledge was his Land Grant
College Bill, which Lincoln signed into
law in 1862. In this April 20, 1858, speech
Morrill promoted the bill, known as the
Morrill Act after its passage.

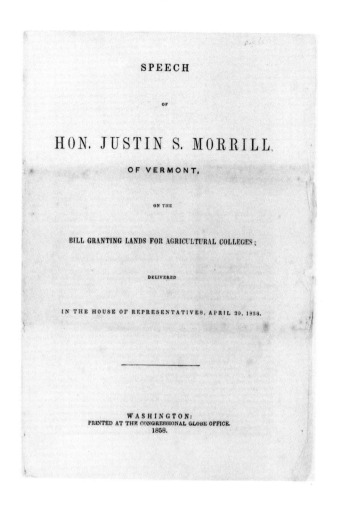

SPEECH

OF

HON. JUSTIN S. MORRILL,

OF VERMONT,

ON THE

BILL GRANTING LANDS FOR AGRICULTURAL COLLEGES;

DELIVERED

IN THE HOUSE OF REPRESENTATIVES, APRIL 20, 1858.

WASHINGTON:
PRINTED AT THE CONGRESSIONAL GLOBE OFFICE.
1858.

Speech on the Land Grant College Bill

downward state of agriculture" in the United States. To him it was a "humiliating fact that we are far in the rear of the best husbandry in Europe," where "agricultural chemistry" raised the productivity of land with innovations like the use of guano, "proving that the fabled eggs of the golden goose have been eclipsed in value by the 'evacuations of seagulls.'"

To revive American agriculture, to give American farmers the knowledge "to raise two blades of grass instead of one," Morrill proposed that the Congress grant to the states twenty thousand acres of land (later raised to thirty thousand) for each Senator and Representative in Congress. The proceeds from the sale of these lands would be a "perpetual" fund, the interest of which must be used to endow at least one college per state "to teach such branches of learning as are related to agriculture and the mechanic arts." Morrill's "land grant college" bill, as it came to be known, passed both houses of Congress but was vetoed by President Buchanan in February 1859, causing its author to lament that "the telegraphic news of the veto will start a tear from the eyes of more than one manly boy, whose ambition will now be nipped in the bud."

With a new administration in office Morrill reintroduced his bill on December 16, 1861, and President Lincoln signed it on July 2, 1862. Six weeks earlier Lincoln had approved a bill creating, as a kind of ally of the land grant colleges, a Department of Agriculture, whose mission was "to acquire and diffuse among the people of the United States useful information on subjects connected with agriculture." The first commissioner of agriculture was Isaac Newton, a Pennsylvania dairy farmer whose passion for research approached that of his namesake. Newton died of a stroke in July 1866, caused by trying to save experimental wheat samples from a thunderstorm. He gave the Department of Agriculture, which achieved cabinet status in 1889, a "research and educational bent" that continues to the present day.

In the years after 1862 Justin Morrill cautioned against shortchanging the mechanical and engineering arts by overemphasizing the agricultural aspect of the land grant colleges. "Agricultural Colleges," Morrill claimed, "would never have been applied to the institutions except that it had happened to suit the casual convenience of an index clerk." As a Senator (which he became in 1866), Morrill continued to be an advocate for higher education, obtaining in 1890 the passage of the so-called second Morrill Act, which gave annual subsidies to the institutions founded under the 1862 act.

Fifty years after the passage of the first Morrill Act there were sixty-eight land grant colleges, enrolling 72,865 students, taught by 5,618 faculty members. Some of these colleges might have been founded (as a few were) without federal encouragement, but the Morrill Act was unquestionably the stimulus for the national network of public institutions of higher learning which other nations are still trying to emulate. "These colleges will go on so long as our nation lives," wrote the Michigan Agricultural College

**College Hall,
Michigan Agricultural College, 1856**
Photograph
Courtesy of Michigan State University

Many land grant colleges rose directly from the forest. Seen here is Michigan Agricultural College, now Michigan State University, which served as a model for numerous colleges built under the Morrill Act. Michigan Agricultural College began as a state-supported school, but it received funding from the Morrill Act after the bill was passed.

(now Michigan State University) *Record* in 1896, and "remain perpetual
monuments to the noble far-seeing Senator; monuments more enduring
than if builded of granite from the hills of the state he represents."

During his distinguished career Justin Morrill raised other enduring
monuments, notably, the Library of Congress, for he was one of the moving
spirits in the construction of the Main (now Jefferson) Building of the Library and in the expansive conception of the Library's role in the promotion
of knowledge which that structure represents. Congress established a Library when it moved to Washington, appropriating five thousand dollars on
April 24, 1800, for "such books as are necessary" for its use. Located in the
Capitol, the Library's books were used for kindling by the British soldiers
who burned the building in 1814. To the rescue came Thomas Jefferson,
who sold his library to Congress in 1815, claiming that it contained no
"branch of science which Congress would wish to exclude from their collections; there is, in fact, no subject to which a Member of Congress may not

have occasion to refer." For the next few decades the Library quietly went about its business, a peaceful oasis in a political cockpit. But it had so little influence beyond Washington that an 1864 *Harper's Magazine* survey of leading American libraries did not mention it.

Change came in 1865 with the appointment of a new Librarian of Congress, Ainsworth Rand Spofford. For a variety of reasons, including the passage of a new copyright law, the Library quickly outgrew its quarters and began to assume the aspects of a national library, a mission Spofford supported. So, too, did powerful members of Congress like "the Tall Sycamore of the Wabash"—Senator Daniel Voorhees of Indiana—and the future "Czar" of the House—Thomas B. Reed—and, of course, Morrill. Beginning in 1871 these men urged their colleagues to erect a separate building to enable the Library to house its mushrooming collections, fast becoming an unmanageable and "futile heap," and to discharge its broadening responsibilities to promote knowledge on a national scale. Warned Senator Morrill in 1879:

> The unyielding truth is that we have got to move Congress out to give room to the Library, or move the Library out to give room for Congress. We must . . . either reduce the Library to the stinted and specific wants of Congress alone, or permit it to advance to national importance, and give it room equal to the culture, wants, and resources of a great people.

Such pleas by Morrill and others, repeated in season and out, had their effect with the result that on April 15, 1886, Congress passed a bill, appropriating funds for a Library of Congress building. Various designs were submitted, including one requiring that the dome of the Capitol be raised fifty feet and the Library inserted in the vacant space. The Congress settled on an "Italian renaissance" structure with the happy results that can be observed today. In its new quarters, augmented by two twentieth-century buildings and strengthened by the Congressional Research Service (founded in 1914 as the Legislative Reference Service), the Library has surmounted the either-or dilemma posed by Morrill in 1879, for it is now able to serve the needs of both the Congress and the nation.

The evolution of the Library of Congress into the National Library was not inevitable; for some years during the middle of the nineteenth century the mantle seemed more likely to fall on the Smithsonian Institution. News that the illegitimate half-brother of the British commander at Lexington in 1775, one James Smithson, had bequeathed to the United States $500,000 to found "an Establishment for the increase and diffusion of knowledge among men" took the nation by surprise in 1835. Pleading want of power, President Jackson asked Congress to administer Smithson's gift. Competing proposals surfaced in both houses and the members spent eleven years deciding what to do. Senator Choate of Massachusetts favored the "purchase of a great national library," as long as it was not selected "by a mere bibliomaniac." Others favored a botanical garden, a national university, and a national museum. John Quincy Adams, for ten years chairman of the

The photograph shows a sign reading:

EOPLE OF MADISON!
VETS IN TENT
EED ROOMS TO RENT
OFFER YOUR SPARE ROOM! GIVE A VET
A CHANCE TO USE THE 'GI BILL.
CALL UNIV. HOUSING BUREAU
BADGER 580

Vets in Tents
Photograph, 1947
Courtesy of the State Historical Society
of Wisconsin

Despite valiant efforts, many colleges and universities were hard-pressed to house World War II veterans seeking education under the G.I. Bill. These "vets" at the University of Wisconsin had obviously learned something about public relations during their military service.

House's special Smithsonian committee, had two objectives: to prevent politicians from wasting the money—"no sinecures, no monkish stalls for lazy idlers"—and to construct a "lighthouse of the skies," as he called his pet project, a national observatory. Eventually, the choice narrowed to an observatory or a museum and after Adams and the astronomy lobby were appeased with a congressional appropriation for a Naval Observatory in 1842, Congress passed an act in 1846 using Smithson's bequest to build a museum. Despite the Smithsonian Institution's immediate success in the dissemination of scientific knowledge, Congress did not turn to its staff when it wanted to establish a body of scientific advisers; rather, through the efforts of Senator Henry Wilson, it created a group of experts outside the government by chartering the National Academy of Sciences in 1863. In the years since, Congress has supported institutions as diverse as the National Institutes of Health and the Government Printing Office, all united by a common mission to promote knowledge.

Knowledge can be promoted by investing in people as well as in buildings, as Congress demonstrated in the 1940s. Assistance to individuals began on a large scale with the Service Readjustment Act of 1944, better known as the G.I. Bill of Rights, which Congress passed to provide money and services to World War II veterans attending college. Despite the predictions of educational experts that an influx of subsidized soldiers would turn American universities into "educational hobo jungles," the G.I. Bill was an unqualified success. After an initial adjustment in stipends, there were few complaints, even though veterans and their families were obliged to live in jerry-built housing without running water, in gymnasiums, in locker rooms, and even on tugboats.

Assistance to individuals did not stop with veterans, however. The Fulbright-Hays Act of 1946, the brainchild of Senator J. William Fulbright, underwrote an international educational and scholarly exchange program. The National Defense Education Act of 1958, a project of Senator Lister Hill and others, provided support to students at various levels of the nation's educational system. While Congress cannot claim sole credit for the National Endowments for the Arts and for the Humanities, both established in 1965, these organizations operate, in general, on the principle of encouraging knowledge by offering financial assistance to individuals and groups. As a sequel to the 1965 Higher Education Act, the Educational Amendments of 1972 provoked a debate over the competing claims on public funding of people and buildings which was resolved in favor of the former through the creation of the Basic Education Opportunity Grants, known as the Pell grants in honor of their sponsor, Senator Claiborne Pell of Rhode Island.

It is often forgotten that there is a presumption in the Constitution that Congress will promote knowledge. Article 1, Section 8, vests in Congress the power "to promote the Progress of Science and useful Arts, by securing for limited Times to Authors and Inventors the exclusive Right to their respective Writings and Discoveries." The Framers expected Congress to use this power to provide patent and copyright protection for American citizens. It has been argued that establishing short-term monopolies with prospects for financial rewards (which is what patents and copyrights do) promotes neither science nor the arts because the true creator is not motivated by money. Thomas Jefferson disagreed, arguing in reference to the patent law that "ingenuity should receive liberal encouragement" which would be "a spring to invention." Sharing Jefferson's view, Congress passed Copyright and Patent Acts in 1790. In 1836 Senator John Ruggles of Maine, himself an inventor, pushed through a revision of the Patent Law which laid the foundations of the system we have today. Ruggles then received Patent Number 1 under the new law for an "improvement in locomotives." The Copyright Act of 1790 required the U.S. District Courts to handle copyright, an unsatisfactory delegation of responsibility, as events proved. Congress revised the system periodically, at last centralizing it in the Library of

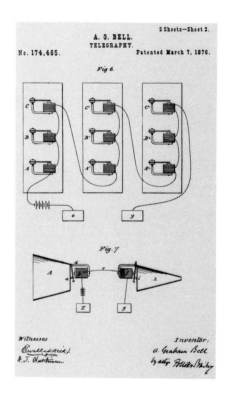

Telegraphy Patent, March 7, 1876
Photograph
Alexander Graham Bell Papers,
Manuscript Division

The Patent Act, passed by Congress in 1790 and revised in 1836, assisted in the promotion of knowledge by securing the rights of inventors to their creations. Alexander Graham Bell's patent model for the telephone was issued in 1876.

Suspenders Anyone?
Label, 1871(?)
Manuscript Division

The Copyright Act of 1870 was a boon to the Library of Congress because it required the deposit in the Library of two copies of every book registered for copyright. An unwelcome aspect of the act was the requirement that the Librarian of Congress grant copyright protection to commercial labels, promoting everything from patent medicine to paint and including suspenders, seen here.

Congress (1870) and establishing a Register of Copyrights in the Library (1897).

Some members of the Philadelphia Convention tried but failed to give Congress the power to grant "rewards" and "premiums" for the "advancement of useful knowledge and discoveries." Congress, nevertheless, has found ways to encourage projectors and inventors, none with happier results than Samuel F. B. Morse. Overcoming wisecracking members who equated electromagnetism with mesmerism and millerism (a religious fad), Congress in 1843 granted thirty thousand dollars to Morse for what we today would call a demonstration project, a trial of the telegraph between Washington and Baltimore. On May 24, 1844, from an office in the Capitol, Morse tapped out his famous message, "What hath God wrought," but the success of his invention was assured by the impact on members of Congress of its instantaneous reporting of the startling events at that year's Democratic National Convention. Meeting in Baltimore, the Democrats rejected the favorite, Martin Van Buren, considered Lewis Cass, and then began dallying with a "dark horse," James K. Polk of Tennessee. As these events unfolded and were reported to members of Congress by Morse from his Capitol Hill office, legislative business stopped and members crowded around Morse to hear the latest word. News of Polk's victory on the ninth ballot was greeted by three congressional cheers for the nominee and three for Morse. The inventor was now a celebrity and his telegraph a sensation.

An excited newspaper reporter claimed that Morse's achievement was "not only an era in the transmission of intelligence, but it has originated in the mind . . . a new species of consciousness." Altering states of consciousness, some would argue, is the business of gurus, not legislators, but over the years Congress, as in the Morse case, has been willing to take chances to promote knowledge and has often received handsome—and unexpected—returns.

Lewis and Clark

Hand-drawn map by Robert Frazer, 1807
Geography and Map Division

One of the first and greatest of American "voyages of discovery," the Lewis and Clark expedition was proposed to Congress by Thomas Jefferson in 1803. Pvt. Robert Frazer drew this map as a member of the expedition.

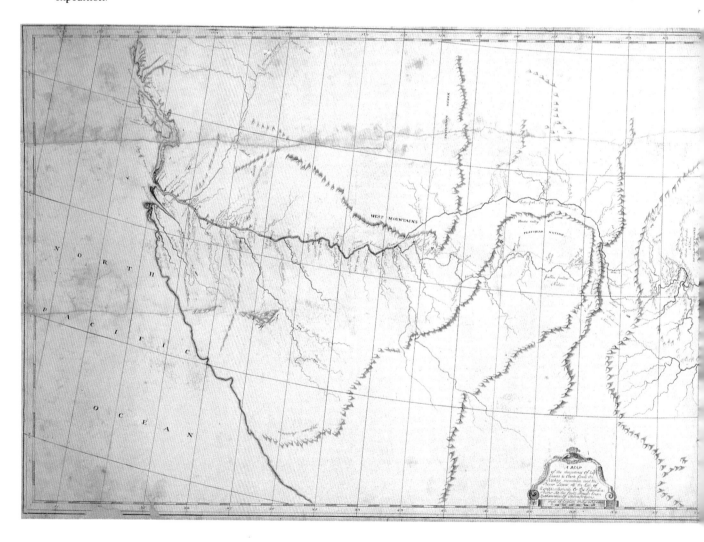

VOYAGES OF DISCOVERY

☆ ☆ ☆ ☆ ☆ ☆ ☆ ☆ ☆ ☆ ☆

Knowledge can be promoted in several ways. Schools can be built and students sent to them. Playing for higher stakes, societies can support experimenters and explorers in hopes that they will make discoveries that will expand the body of knowledge itself. It was an effort of this second sort that Thomas Jefferson commended to Congress in his secret message of January 18, 1803, proposing an exploration of the "river Missouri . . . even to the Western ocean." The United States, Jefferson asserted, "should enlarge the boundaries of knowledge by undertaking voyages of discovery." From Lewis and Clark to Armstrong and Aldrin, from the Rocky Mountains to the mountains of the moon, Congress has accepted Jefferson's challenge and has supported American explorers on their voyages of discovery.

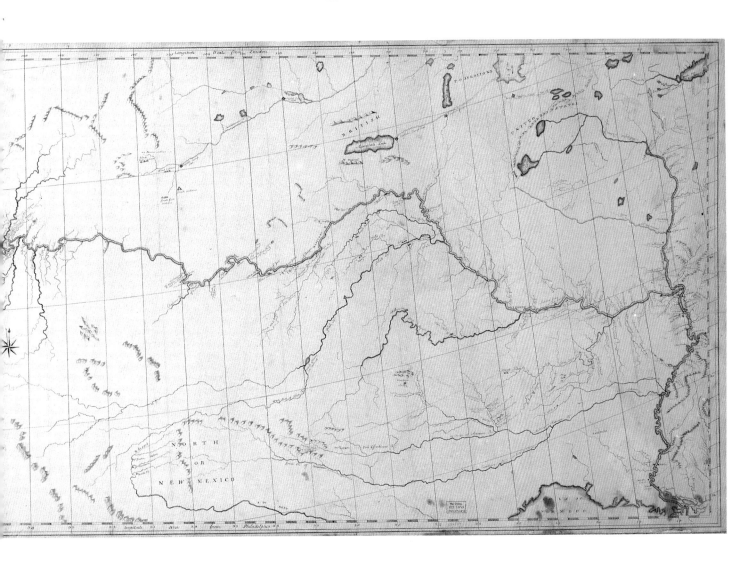

There has been a pattern to congressional support of exploration, as John Wesley Powell, the conqueror of the Grand Canyon, explained in 1878: "It should be remembered," wrote Powell, "that the statesmen of America who compose and have composed our National Legislature have not been adverse to the endowment of scientific research" and exploration when they are "properly related to the industries of the people." Powell meant that Congress had a record of supporting exploration that was useful to the country's citizens. Impatient at first with any venture that did not yield an immediate payoff, Congress soon took a more indulgent attitude toward exploration and permitted "pure" scientific projects to flourish under its wing. In our own time Congress has underwritten the most ambitious and most scientifically rewarding of all American voyages of discovery, the exploration of space.

The Lewis and Clark expedition was the model for congressionally supported exploration in the nineteenth century. It was sold to Congress by Jefferson on practical grounds—as an effort to bring the western fur trade under American control—and it was justified, as all nineteenth-century exploring and scientific enterprises were, by invoking Congress's power to regulate commerce. Risky though Lewis and Clark's reconnaissance of Indian country was, an early nineteenth-century voyage along the American coastline could be equally so, because American territorial waters were as uncharted as the western wilderness. As late as 1828 Secretary of the Navy Samuel Southard complained that maritime maps were "unsafe and in many instances, useless and pernicious," a fact attested by the annual toll of shipwrecks. To promote safer shipping, Congress appropriated fifty thousand dollars in 1807 for a survey of American coasts and waters "within 20 leagues of the shore." Not until 1816, however, was a superintendent appointed for the United States Coast Survey—a prickly mathematician named Ferdinand Rudolph Hassler. Hassler conceived the Coast Survey to be a scientific expedition requiring the most careful and deliberate planning and staffing. Wanting quick results and receiving none, Congress dismissed the superintendent in 1818 and "suspended" the Coast Survey.

In 1826 Representative Gulian Verplanck of New York moved the revival of the survey and in 1832 Hassler, though attacked as an "old Swiss . . . who writes a miserable jargon which he calls English and scolds like a fish fag," was rehired. This time Congress was more patient and generous with Hassler, granting the survey an appropriation which reached $100,000 annually by 1840. Congress's generosity was owing, in no small measure, to the discovery by one of Hassler's hydrologists of a new channel in New York harbor, which was a boon to shipping. In 1843 Hassler was succeeded by Benjamin Franklin's great-grandson, Alexander Dallas Bache, an accomplished scientist who knew his way around Washington and could easily parry charges that Coast Survey employees were using the agency's ships as "headquarters for frolicking." Under Bache the Coast Survey became the premier scientific agency in the federal government. It explored and mapped the Pacific Coast to assist the growing American commerce there

New York Harbor, 1845
Chart, United States Coast Survey
Geography and Map Division

The United States Coast Survey prepared the first accurate maps of many of the nation's harbors. The survey discovered a new channel in New York harbor, which endeared it to the shipping industry.

AN
EXPLORING EXPEDITION
ON THE
CANAL STREET PLAN.

Respectfully inscribed to
Army, and the Board of Navy

I think that the Board are certainly at Sea now!—

Navy Commissioners
Pap Bowl.

Gotham

THE
EXPLORING EXPEDITION
AT THE
SOUTH POLE,
WAITING FOR STORES.

the Secretaries of the Navy and
Commissioners, by

their humble servant

Robinson Crusoe

and with Congress's acquiescence conducted investigations of "exotic" subjects like terrestrial magnetism and coral formation in the Florida Keys.

The Pacific Ocean interested Americans long before Bache took over at the Coast Survey. In 1828 the House passed a bill authorizing an exploration of the "western ocean," principally as a result of the lobbying of Jeremiah Reynolds, at one time a disciple of John Cleves Symmes, an American army officer acclaimed by some simple-minded countrymen as "the Newton of the West" because of his theory that the earth was a series of concentric spheres, open at the poles, and "hollow and habitable" within. The Senate rejected the Pacific exploration bill in 1829, but Reynolds continued to promote it, promising that it would bring into existence new industries—a trade in exotic bird feathers, for example. Reynolds also enlisted the support of whaling and sealing interests, looking for new killing grounds, and of organizations like the East India Marine Society of Salem, Massachusetts, which memorialized Congress that commerce was suffering because of ignorance of places like the "Feejee or Beetee Islands," where crews were wrecking on reefs and being massacred by natives. Pressure from such groups was successful, and Congress in 1836 appropriated $150,000 with authority to use another $150,000 in navy funds for the United States Exploring Expedition, popularly known as the Ex Ex or as the Wilkes Expedition after its commander, Lt. Charles Wilkes. More indulgent toward science than twenty years earlier when it dismissed Hassler, Congress made

The Exploring Expedition
Engraving, 1838
Prints and Photographs Division

In 1836 Congress funded the United States Exploring Expedition. The bureaucratic infighting and personal jealousies which delayed the departure of the "Ex Ex" for two years are satirized here. The forlorn explorers waiting for stores at the South Pole are surrounded by polar bears, which do not exist in Antarctica.

provisons for a "corp of scientific men" to accompany the expedition, even though it was frankly told that "in matters of science utility cannot be computed in advance." Delayed for two years by infighting among the participants, the Wilkes Expedition left Norfolk, Virginia, in August 1838 and sailed the world's seas for four years, confirming that Antarctica was a continent and sending back scientific samples in such abundance that they overwhelmed storage facilities in Washington. Its map of Tarawa was a belated rebuke to those who questioned the practical value of scientific exploration, for it was used by the United States Marine Corps in its invasion of that island in 1943.

How were the results of the Ex Ex to be disseminated? Senator Benjamin Tappan of Ohio, in his spare time an "eager conchologist," arranged for the Joint Committee on the Library of Congress to publish the expedition's reports, and it dutifully brought the volumes out, incurring printing costs as late as 1872. Thus, "the greatest scientific publishing project undertaken by the government before the Civil War was directly under Congress."

Some members of Congress opposed the Wilkes Expedition, claiming that instead of traipsing around Tahiti, Americans should be exploring their own country first. In the 1850s much of the trans-Mississippi West was still unknown, a fact that did not dampen the growing enthusiasm for a transcontinental railroad. Each section of the country had its favorite route, incontestably superior to all others. Competitors could expect no quarter from rival promoters. Favoring a central route, as any Missouri man would, Senator Thomas Hart Benton blasted the southwestern route as "so utterly desolate, desert, and God-forsaken that Kit Carson says a wolf could not

The Great Morai of Temarre
Drawing by Titian Peale, 1839
Manuscript Division

Congress authorized the United States Exploring Expedition to employ a "corp of scientific men," among whom was the artist Titian Peale. On Tahiti in September 1839 Peale sketched this morai, built of coral block, resembling the "pyramids of Mexico." According to Peale, the morai was 40 feet high, 20 feet wide at the top, and 50 feet wide at the base.

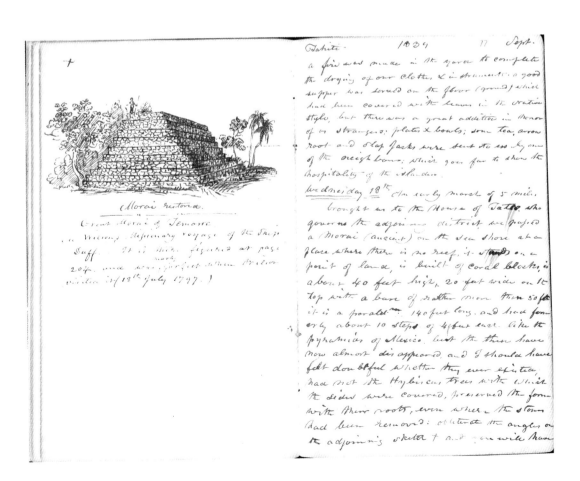

Stanley.Del.   Sarony, Major & Knapp, Lith. 449 Broadway,N.Y

make his living on it." Deadlocked over route selection, Congress in 1853 adopted a proposal of Senators Richard Brodhead and William Gwin which amounted to submitting the problem to scientific arbitration—expeditions would be sent into different parts of the West and their reports would be used to pick the best path to the Pacific. Following the Wilkes example, each expedition was accompanied by scientists who studied everything from ornithology to the social structure of Indian tribes. Topographical information was, of course, the first priority and voluminous reports were submitted about the terrain and national resources along each route. After the railroad surveys had done their work, the country was no longer ignorant of western geography. But geographers and scientists were no match for sectional passions and no Pacific railroad could be built until the South seceded from the Union and broke the political deadlock in Congress.

The free and easy politics of post-Civil War America, which enriched the grafters and the crooks, was also beneficial to science and exploration. In fact, there was excess here, as in other sectors of American life. During the Grant administration Congress simultaneously supported four western exploring expeditions. There was duplication of effort and few should have been surprised when parties from two expeditions bumped into each other in Colorado in 1874, creating a "scandal," tame by Gilded Age standards, which required Congress's attention.

Clarence King, a young man on a track so fast that Henry Adams compared him to Alexander the Great, started the ball rolling in 1867 by persuading Congress to underwrite his Geological Survey of the Fortieth Parallel. Promoting the survey as a means of assessing America's mineral wealth, King relied on the influence of Senator John Conness, after whom he had had the foresight to name a mountain he had climbed earlier in California. Following the Wilkes model, King took along a contingent of scientists. Of more immediate value to the public than King's geological investigations was his exposure in 1872 of the great Diamond Hoax, a fraud perpetrated on San Francisco banking interests by two con men who seeded a field in northwest Colorado with cheap gems bought in Europe.

Another enterprising geologist, John Wesley Powell, used his influence with the Illinois congressional delegation to secure support in 1869 for an exploration of the Grand Canyon, "the last completely blank area on the country's map." In the same year Lt. George Wheeler began military mapping expeditions in Nevada and Utah. Not to be outdone, the General Land Office persuaded Congress to back Ferdinand Hayden's survey of the public domain in the Rocky Mountain area. It was Hayden's and Wheeler's men who stumbled into each other in 1874, a collision that prompted a movement in Congress, under the leadership of Representatives Abram Hewitt and James Garfield, to consolidate the various surveys into the United States Geological Survey, which was done in 1879. Although it would be an exaggeration to say that by that date Americans knew everything they always wanted to know about the West, three decades of crisscrossing the area and probing its nooks and crannies, under congressional sponsorship, had solved all of its major mysteries. There was, as Powell said in 1874, "now left within . . . the United States no great unexplored region and exploring expeditions are no longer needed for general purposes."

But voyages of discovery were far from finished. The ends of the earth beckoned adventurous men and Americans answered the call. They took the lead in trying to reach the North Pole, but not with congressional

Coste's Hummingbird
From Pacific Railroad Reports, *vol. 10*
(1857)
General Collections

Like the Ex Ex, the Pacific railroad surveys received congressional funding to employ scientists. Many unfamiliar species of birds and animals were encountered along the various routes. Coste's hummingbird, found first in New Mexico along the thirty-fifth parallel in February 1854, was one of these.

support. A spot on a frozen ocean, the pole offered, as far as anyone could tell, no tangible returns on an investment to reach it; therefore, expeditions were supported by wealthy, armchair explorers—"kitchen geographers," as one critic called them. During the first week of September 1909 each of the American rivals, Frederick A. Cook and Robert E. Peary, announced that he had become the first person to reach the Pole. A furious debate about the priority of discovery erupted between the partisans of the explorers which continues to the present day. Congress held hearings on the controversy in 1910–11 and 1915–16 in which its role was the reverse of what it had been in the 1850s. Then, explorers were commissioned to solve a political problem; now politicians were trying to resolve an explorers' problem. "The American Eagle," asserted Cook, "has spread its wings of glory over the Worlds Top. Whether there is room for one or two under those wings is a question upon which Dr. Cook asks a National Decision—write your Congressman." Given the conflicting evidence, Congress returned the Scotch verdict of not proven. On March 4, 1911, it adopted a resolution merely thanking Peary for "reaching the North Pole," leaving open the question of who reached the pole first. Some have argued that neither Cook nor Peary reached the Pole and that the first person to do so later served as

Natural Column, Washakie Badlands, Wyoming
From Report of the Geological Exploration of the Fortieth Parallel (1870–80)
General Collections

Clarence King's fortieth parallel survey, along which this natural column was seen, was one of several western surveys commissioned by Congress after the Civil War.

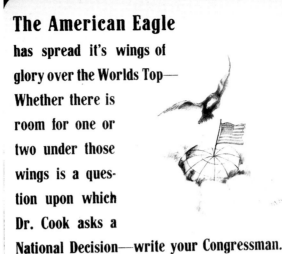

The American Eagle

has spread it's wings of glory over the Worlds Top—Whether there is room for one or two under those wings is a question upon which Dr. Cook asks a National Decision—write your Congressman.

**The American Eagle
Has Spread Its Wings**

*Glass lantern slide, 1909
Prints and Photographs Division
Peary photograph courtesy of the
National Archives and Records
Administration
Cook photograph copyright
© Helene Cook Vetter 1951;
reprinted by permission of Janet Vetter*

In September 1909 a dispute arose between Arctic explorers Robert Peary (right) and Frederick Cook (left) over who had first discovered the North Pole. The controversy cannot yet be said to have been settled. The question of priority of discovery was investigated by Congress in 1910–11 and again in 1915–16. Cook prepared this announcement in advance of one of those investigations in an effort to rally public support behind his cause.

a member of Congress, William R. Anderson, who as commander of the atomic submarine *Nautilus*, passed under the pole on August 3, 1958.

Modern technology has carried explorers to areas far more forbidding than the North Pole. Space itself has become a venue for voyages of discovery. The beep, beep of Sputnik I, the world's first artificial satellite, launched by the Soviet Union on October 4, 1957, jolted a complacent American public into demanding a comparable effort in space. The Eisenhower administration, with a powerful boost from Senator Lyndon Johnson, responded by enacting on July 29, 1958, the National Aeronautics and Space Act, which created a new civilian agency, NASA, to run the American space program.

Congress supported the space program because the American people felt that the nation's security required it, that the Soviets could not be permitted to monopolize new technologies which would give them scientific and, perhaps, military superiority over the United States. After the Russians put Yuri Gagarin into earth orbit, April 12, 1961, congressional concern that the American program catch up with the Soviets was so strong that space agency officials were "hard put to restrain Congress from forcing more money on NASA than could be effectively used." Lt. Col. John H. Glenn, Jr., now Senator from Ohio, became the first American to orbit the earth on February 20, 1962, but Congress would not be satisfied until NASA achieved the greatest voyage of discovery in human history—Apollo 11's landing of Neil Armstrong and Edwin Aldrin on the moon on July 20, 1969.

As dramatic as the moon landing was, unmanned satellites and probes have learned more about space than human explorers. NASA's Pioneers, Mariners, and Voyagers have discovered the earth's radiation belts, its magnetosphere, and solar wind. They have confirmed the existence of black holes and have produced detailed profiles of our planetary neighbors. Ever mindful of the American habit of demanding practical payoffs from exploration, NASA had by 1973 identified and publicized thirty thousand items of space technology which could be converted to civilian use. Still, recent years have witnessed a simmering public impatience with "pure" space exploration, to which Congress has responded by reducing appropriations for some projects. But, by swiftly coming to NASA's rescue after the *Challenger* disaster, Congress showed that its commitment to the space program remains strong and that voyages of discovery will continue into places that would have been unimaginable to Thomas Jefferson and his generation.

John Glenn
*Photograph, National Aeronautics
and Space Administration, 1961
Manuscript Division*

Lt. Col.—now Senator—John H. Glenn, Jr., in training for his historic orbital flight around the earth, February 20, 1962.

AFTERWORD

"Congress," wrote Woodrow Wilson in 1893, "in its composition is the country in miniature." Wilson meant that the various interests in the nation found their voices in Congress and that Congress was a barometer of the national mood. If Americans were angry with each other, if they raged at each other, as they did in the years before the Civil War, Congress would resemble, in the words of one member, a "Texas bar room." As the country cooled down after 1865, so did Congress. Civility returned and Congress became a kinder, gentler institution.

Over the years Congress also became a stabler institution. Throughout the nineteenth century, turnover, especially in the House, was rapid. Since sessions were short, many members who came to Washington considered themselves rather like tourists, spending their brief stay in the capital as "Scholars in a college or Monks in a monastery, crowded ten or twenty in a house." As tenure and sessions lengthened in the twentieth century, service in Congress began to seem more like a vocation. With lawmaking beginning to resemble a full-time job, Congress participated in a broad trend in American society called professionalization. Regularity of procedures and expertise began to be cherished, staffs were hired to provide these and other services, and buildings and facilities were erected to house staffs. Congress grew, but so did the executive branch, and so did corporate America. If Congress and its support apparatus began to have a bureaucratic flavor, the legislature was merely reflecting developments in all sectors of American life in the twentieth century.

Have Congress's rules and procedures also changed to mirror trends in society? Since the 1960s the country has expended much energy in securing rights and procedural fairness for its citizens and in becoming more "open" and democratic. Congress has not been a laggard in these respects—opening its committees to the public, electing its chairmen, and guaranteeing fairness to citizens who appear before it. It has moved to assure due process to participants in impeachment proceedings, hearings, and investigations. The days of Balie Peyton threatening a witness with a pistol or Joseph McCarthy browbeating a citizen are, it appears, gone forever.

There can be no question that Congress is more efficient than it was in its early days. Legislative business in both houses can now be conducted expeditiously; many weapons of obstruction that the rules once permitted have been spiked. It is in the nature of a partisan body that some members will object to the manner in which the rules and procedures are applied. Congress would not be Congress—indeed, democracy would be in danger—if there were not complaints about how the institution was being run. But the long view yields the conclusion that, although Congress might conduct its business better in the future, it is operating more effectively now than it did in the past.

Was Congress more creative yesterday than it is today? Some might argue that Congress has ceded its primacy in government, that it has relinquished to the executive the role it played in the nineteenth century as the innovative engine of American statecraft. To mention just a few of the seminal acts earlier Congresses passed without any contribution from the executive—the Bill of Rights, the Homestead Act, the Morrill Act, the Yellowstone National Park Act—establishes the high standard against which any twentieth-century Congress must measure itself. Yet it should be remembered that the twentieth century has been almost one continuous crisis—two world wars, a cold war, the Great Depression—which tilts the balance of power in American government in the direction of the executive. It is frequently forgotten that Congress has acquiesced, for patriotic motives, in these developments. The record seems to show that Congress tends to dominate in peaceful, "normal" times and, if these recur, we might experience another era of what Woodrow Wilson called "Congressional Government."

Would the Founding Fathers recognize today's Congress and, if so, would they approve it? The answer is yes in both cases. Some developments would surprise the Framers of the Constitution. They would not have anticipated the high rates at which current House incumbents are being reelected, a trend that creates stability in a chamber the Framers expected to be fickle and turbulent. The popular election of Senators would perplex many of the Framers, who could not reconcile such a fact with ancient, political theories about the upper house. On the other hand, not too much about the mechanics of today's Congress would be foreign to the Framers, for both Houses operate in parliamentary ways, many little changed for centuries, with which a Hamilton or a Madison would be comfortable in no time.

The Framers would approve today's Congress because it is working as they planned. In the famous tenth number of the *Federalist*, James Madison explained that he and his colleagues intended to save republican government by extending its operations over a large area which would include numerous, discordant interest groups. The clashing of these interest groups in Congress would form a system of checks and balances which would prevent any of them from establishing a tyrannical ascendancy over all others. Out of the clashing interaction of interest groups Madison believed would issue measures serving the public good.

This is a picture of what has happened in Congress. It is an arena in which the nation's diverse interests, embodied in the members, have contended for two hundred years; these interests successive generations of members have managed in such a way as to prevent tyranny and promote the public welfare. To have preserved free government and a prosperous society for two centuries during which time legislative bodies around the world have been routinely ignored, obliterated, and converted into rubber stamps for dictators is a remarkable achievement, one of which the Congress of the United States can be enormously proud—and for which its constituents can be enormously grateful.